At Issue

Genetically
Modified Food

Other Books in the At Issue Series:

At Issue

Genetically Modified Food

Tamara Thompson, Book Editor

GREENHAVEN PRESS
A part of Gale, Cengage Learning

GALE
CENGAGE Learning·

Farmington Hills, Mich • San Francisco • New York • Waterville, Maine
Meriden, Conn • Mason, Ohio • Chicago

Elizabeth Des Chenes, *Director, Content Strategy*
Douglas Dentino, *Manager, New Product*

© 2015 Greenhaven Press, a part of Gale, Cengage Learning

WCN: 01-100-101

Gale and Greenhaven Press are registered trademarks used herein under license.

For more information, contact:
Greenhaven Press
27500 Drake Rd.
Farmington Hills, MI 48331-3535
Or you can visit our Internet site at gale.cengage.com

For product information and technology assistance, contact us at

Gale Customer Support, 1-800-877-4253
For permission to use material from this text or product, submit all requests online at www.cengage.com/permissions

Further permissions questions can be emailed to permissionrequest@cengage.com

Articles in Greenhaven Press anthologies are often edited for length to meet page requirements. In addition, original titles of these works are changed to clearly present the main thesis and to explicitly indicate the author's opinion. Every effort is made to ensure that Greenhaven Press accurately reflects the original intent of the authors. Every effort has been made to trace the owners of copyrighted material.

Cover image © Images.com/Corbis.

LIBRARY OF CONGRESS CATALOGING-IN-PUBLICATION DATA

Genetically modified food (Greenhaven Press : 2014)
    Genetically modified food / Tamara Thompson, book editor.
        pages cm. -- (At issue)
    Summary: "At Issue: Genetically Modified Food: Books in this anthology series focus a wide range of viewpoints onto a single controversial issue, providing in-depth discussions by leading advocates, a quick grounding in the issues, and a challenge to critical thinking skills"-- Provided by publisher.
    Includes bibliographical references and index.
    ISBN 978-0-7377-7169-5 (hardback) -- ISBN 978-0-7377-7170-1 (paperback)
    1. Genetically modified foods. 2. Food--Biotechnology. 3. Transgenic plants. 4. Crops--Genetic engineering. I. Thompson, Tamara, editor. II. Title.
    TP248.65.F66G45746 2014
    664--dc23
                                                                2014019391

Printed in the United States of America
1 2 3 4 5   19 18 17 16 15

Contents

Introduction

Reading about genetically modified (GM) food can sometimes feel like trying to make sense of alphabet soup. The acronyms GM, GE (genetically engineered), and GMO (genetically modified organism) are all used interchangeably when discussing the issue, and GM, GE, or GMO foods may also be referred to as transgenic, bioengineered, or biotech foods or crops. Underneath the varied terminology, however, all these words describe the same thing: taking a gene from one type of organism and adding it to the DNA of another in order to introduce a new trait that does not naturally occur in the species.

Since the first GM food crop, the Flavr Savr tomato, was introduced just twenty years ago, it has become commonplace to grow crops from bioengineered seeds all over the world. Today's GM food crops are designed to resist certain pests or diseases, make them more drought tolerant or less prone to spoilage, or even to be more nutritious.

Among the GM plant varieties with special attributes now being grown are potatoes that produce their own pesticides; corn engineered to withstand Monsanto Company's Roundup weed-killer; squash and papayas that resist viruses; and Golden Rice, a rice augmented with beta carotene to help offset potentially deadly vitamin A deficiencies in undernourished populations worldwide. A genetically modified fish, the AquAdvantage salmon, has been engineered to grow twice as fast as regular salmon and is nearing approval from the US Food and Drug Administration (FDA); it is likely to become the first transgenic food animal approved for human consumption.

Most Americans are unaware that they probably already eat genetically modified foods every day. The US Department of Agriculture estimates that 90 percent of US soybeans, sugar beets, and corn is genetically modified, and food ingredients made from those crops—such as high fructose corn syrup, dextrose, soy lecithin, and corn starch—are found in most processed and packaged foods, sodas, and cereals. Corn is also a staple for animal feed, so most US-grown meat is raised on a diet of GM grain as well. By many estimates, 80 percent of the American food supply contains some form of GMO.

Indeed, genetically modified crops are ubiquitous in the United States and the country is the largest global producer of them, accounting for 40 percent of the GM crop acres planted worldwide. Much of that cropland is planted with seeds developed by Monsanto, the largest and most well-known of the big agricultural biotechnology companies. To say that Monsanto shapes global agricultural policy and practice would be an understatement; more often than not, it outright defines it with its formidable technologies, business tactics, and political and economic clout.

According to the International Service for the Acquisition of Agri-biotech Applications (ISAAA), an international non-profit that promotes biotechnology, Monsanto controls 80 percent of the GM corn market and 93 percent of the GM soy market in the United States; that translates to 72 percent and 84 percent of the nation's total harvest of corn and soy, respectively. Forty percent of the country's total cropland (more than 151 million acres) was planted with Monsanto crops in 2013. Worldwide, a record 433 million acres of GM crops were grown in 2013 by eighteen million farmers; a staggering 282 million of those acres—65 percent—were planted with Monsanto crops. The company owns 1,676 patents for seeds, plants, herbicides, and other agricultural products.

Because Monsanto is such a major player in the global biotech industry, it has also become the prime target for those who oppose the development of genetically modified foods, and the company has been heavily vilified by the anti-GMO movement. Critics not only argue that GM crops in general are unsafe to eat and harmful to the environment, but that widespread dependence on Monsanto's GM seeds in particular gives the company too much power over the global food supply. That concern is underscored, they say, because the company sells seeds engineered with "terminator" genes that produce plants that are sterile. That means new seeds must be repurchased each year from the company rather than being saved by farmers, an ancient practice on which farmers worldwide rely for the next year's planting.

Monsanto maintains the sterile seeds are essential to protect its technology patents and keep its intellectual property from being spread around the globe without payment. Its GM seeds, the company says, allow farmers to significantly increase their yields per acre and help address global hunger. Ironically, critics fear that restricting access to the means of food production via sterile seeds could instead threaten the stability of the world's food supply, especially in developing countries that are increasingly turning to higher-yielding GM crops. According to ISAAA, in 2013, developing countries grew more GM crops than industrial countries did for the second year in a row. Latin American, Asian, and African farmers collectively grew 54 percent of GM crops worldwide.

Rallying around this and other concerns, on May 25, 2013, up to two million protesters in 436 cities and fifty-two countries around the world took to the streets for a global "March Against Monsanto" to protest the company's seed practices and GMOs in general. Although it was the largest anti-GMO protest in US history, it was less unusual for other countries, which have been much more reluctant to accept GMOs in their food supplies. Europe in particular has a long history of opposing genetically modified foods—or "frankenfoods" as Europeans are fond of calling them—and the European Union (EU) has some of the strictest GMO regulations in the world.

Despite broad scientific consensus that GM foods pose no greater risk than conventionally grown foods, and the fact that no negative health effects have ever been documented in humans from eating them, sixty-four countries—including the EU, Brazil, Australia, Japan, and China—require foods containing GMO ingredients to be specifically labeled.

In the United States, the FDA does not recognize any difference between GM and non-GM foods (neither plants nor animals), and it maintains that federally mandated labeling is not necessary because GM foods have the same essential characteristics of nutrition and composition as their non-GM counterparts. Likewise, the biotech industry argues that requiring labels would improperly imply a warning where none is justified.

The US public is skeptical though, and the sentiment has gone mainstream; a 2013 poll by the *New York Times* showed that 93 percent of Americans want foods that contain GMOs labeled. Ballot measures to require GMO labeling in California and Washington barely failed to pass in 2012 and 2013, respectively, even though the biotech and processed food industries spent a whopping $70 million to oppose the initiatives. Connecticut and Maine became the first states to pass mandatory GMO labeling laws in 2013, but both have so-called trigger clauses that require four other states with a combined population of more than twenty million to enact similar measures before they can take effect.

That quorum may be on its way, however. On May 8, 2014, Vermont's governor signed the nation's first "no strings attached" law requiring the labeling of genetically modified foods. All genetically modified organisms and foods containing any GM ingredient must be labeled in Vermont by July 2016.

With the FDA widely expected to approve the AquAdvantage salmon sometime in 2014, however, more than three dozen states are currently organizing GMO labeling initiatives, and several are expected to make the 2014 ballot, according to the Non-GMO Project, a nonprofit that certifies GMO-free foods.

In the meantime, in the absence of labels, the only way American consumers can know for sure whether their food is genetically modified or not is to buy organic products or look for labels indicating that a product does *not* contain GMOs. As public awareness about the prevalence of GM foods has grown and American consumers have become more engaged around their food choices, such labels have become increasingly common on supermarket shelves.

The authors in *At Issue: Genetically Modified Food* represent a wide range of viewpoints concerning the potential benefits and consequences—both to human health and the environment—of developing and consuming genetically modified plants and animals.

1

Why Are Genetically Modified Foods Controversial?

Eric Siegel

Eric Siegel wrote this viewpoint for the campus newspaper, The Tufts Daily, *when he was a student at Tufts University. He is currently a marketing associate for Boston Organics.*

Arguments put forth by both sides in the debate over genetically modified (GM) food are based on fear and alarmism rather than on reason and sound science. Those who support the widespread use of GM foods often say they are necessary to combat global population growth and potential mass starvation, while those who oppose GM foods raise alarm over their potential environmental and health risks. Focusing on extremes at either end of the spectrum does a disservice to the conversation about GM foods. In truth, the benefits are just as important as the risks, and it is essential for the public to have access to real, meaningful information so that people can critically examine the issue and form their opinions based on more than just rhetoric.

The public debate over genetically modified (GM) food has devolved into a scrappy shouting match unrooted from the reality of the international food system. The combative dialogue confuses the public and does little to ensure the adoption of transformative policies or technologies that are necessary to fix our broken food system. And our food system is broken—the World Health Organization and Food and Agriculture Organization report that 1.4 billion adults are overweight while 870 million people around the world do not have enough to eat.

Those who support the widespread adoption of GM technology, the manipulation of plant and animal genes to produce more efficient and resilient crops and livestock, cultivate stories of massive overpopulation and wide-scale starvation in a future world without GM food. David Stark, a vice president at [agricultural biotechnology company] Monsanto, spoke at the Friedman School [of Nutrition Science and Policy at Tufts University] last month [March 2013]. Before he articulated the position of one of the world's largest investors in GM technology he told the audience, "If we had the same yields today that we had in 1950, about half of us would starve in this country. Farming continuously improves and that's what we have to be a part of."

> Food companies ... support GM technology because it can make food more resilient and durable, thereby improving shelf life and decreasing waste.

Competing Fears

The other side of the debate harvests our existing mistrust of new technology and spins tales of Frankenstein-food and apocalyptic environmental destruction. The Center for Food Safety, a national public interest group and environmental advocacy organization, writes that "each decision to introduce these biological contaminants into our environment is a dangerous game of ecological roulette. The extent of irreversible environmental damage grows greater with every new acre of GE cropland and every new GE variety." (GE is "genetically engineered" and is used synonymously with GM.)

These two fears—that we won't be able to produce enough food for a growing world population and that the technology we develop in the name of progress will bring about our own destruction—are inherent motivating forces in an industrial food system. Since the French Revolution, regular cycles of gluts and surpluses have caused panic in the western world. The debate over GM foods sounds a lot like the historical arguments over hybrid seeds, chemical pesticides, and tractors. As new technology develops to address a looming food shortage, skepticism that a long-term solution can be found through scientific advancement waxes and wanes in parallel.

While vitriolic rhetoric over the future food supply is hardly new, we can address the problems with our food system more productively if we engage in open, honest discussion over the pros and cons of this new technology known as genetic modification.

A Look at the Benefits

Advocates for the proliferation of GM food, like Monsanto, believe that biotechnology can improve productivity through increased yields and thus bring farmers more income. Climate change activist Mark Lynas insists that GM food means we won't have to clear rainforests to plant more crops. Food companies like Pepsico support GM technology because it can make food more resilient and durable, thereby improving shelf life and decreasing waste. Innovative products like Golden Rice [a genetically modified grain] use biotechnology to improve the nutritional quality of food. Some promote GM food because they believe that GM crops require fewer herbicides and could allow farmers in inclement climates to grow a new variety of crops locally.

Those who seek to prohibit the proliferation of GM food, like the Center for Food Safety, believe that biotechnology can lead to the creation of antibiotic-resistant superbugs. Greenpeace International views GM as a hubristic attempt to conquer nature that results in a loss of biodiversity and damages the resilience of existing ecosystems. Food companies like

Nature's Path and Clif Bar note that pesticide and herbicide use has increased with GM crops. Anti-GM advocates argue that there is a lack of independent research for a technology that is being implemented more quickly than DDT [pesticide banned in United States in 1972]. Farmers can become entangled in a cycle of debt to large agribusinesses as a result of the monopolization of patents and agricultural inputs. GM foods could result in unforeseen allergic responses, though food processors claim to thoroughly test each item before it is sold commercially. While GM might allow farmers to grow new crops in new climates, most locavores advocate for a more historically 'natural' diet that doesn't include GM food. Furthermore, if American farmers are able to grow tropical fruit, the farmers in the global south will no longer have a profitable export market.

Concerns Are Equally Important

The concerns over GM food are as real as the potential benefits. Already 88 percent of corn and 93 percent of soy grown in the United States, the two most widely planted crops, are genetically modified. Although a standard labeling and tracing system has not been implemented, most experts estimate that 70 percent of processed food on a conventional supermarket shelf contains GM material.

For us to truly debate the merits of this technology, we need more information. We don't know when we're eating GM food so we don't know if it makes us sick. We don't know the extent of gene manipulation because profit-driven agribusinesses horde patents and copyrights. We don't know if GM seeds will increase or decrease the amount of pesticides that farmers will use in the future. If we want to slice through the rhetoric we need more transparency, accountability and patience from everyone involved in this conversation.

Before you make up your mind about this revolutionary scientific advancement, before you determine that this is a *deus ex machina* [a person or thing that appears unexpectedly and provides an artificial solution to a seemingly unsolvable problem] or cast it aside as the apple of Eden, before you start investing your money or boycotting companies, before you sign your name to a petition or vote on ballot measure, take a moment to critically examine the technology and its consequences and join a new conversation about genetically modified food.

2

Genetically Modified Foods Are Safe to Eat

Monsanto Company

The Monsanto Company is a US-based multinational agricultural biotechnology corporation. It is the world's leading producer of the herbicide glyphosate, marketed as "Roundup," and one of the largest producers of genetically modified seeds and crops.

Plants and crops that feature genetically modified (GM) traits have been tested more thoroughly than any other crop in the history of agriculture, and there is no credible evidence that they cause harm to humans or animals, or to the environment. Biotech companies, independent scientists, and government regulatory agencies—such as the US Food and Drug Administration, Department of Agriculture, and Environmental Protection Agency—all play important roles in insuring that GM crops are safe to eat and are safe for the environment. Labeling such crops as being genetically modified is not necessary because there is no meaningful difference in safety, composition, or nutrition between GM crops and crops that are traditionally grown. Because of that, there is also no need to test further the safety of biotech crops by doing clinical trials on humans.

In recent years, people have become increasingly interested in where their food comes from and how it is produced. And unfortunately, despite a 20-year record of safety and almost 2,500 independent, global scientific reviews and approvals of GMO [genetically modified organism] crops, there is still conflicting and confusing information about GMOs. We realize you may have questions about the safety of our products, and following are answers to ten of the questions we most commonly receive. Please feel free to contact us with other questions you may have.

What Are Biotechnology, Genetic Engineering, Genetic Modification and GMOs?

We use agricultural biotechnology, or genetic engineering [GE] of plants, to develop new varieties of plant seeds with a range of desirable characteristics, such as being able to resist certain insects or harsh weather conditions.

Genetically modified [GM] crops—also known as genetically modified organisms (GMOs), GE crops or biotech crops—include one or more genes from another organism, such as a bacterium or other microbe or other plant species. For plants, the inserted gene results in a beneficial characteristic in the plant, such as the ability to tolerate environmental pressures from damaging insects or drought. GMO is commonly used to refer to GM plants, as well as the food or ingredients from GM plants.

As a seed company, Monsanto studies, breeds, grows and sells GM seeds—as well as conventional seeds—to farmers around the world. Our research teams use traditional and advanced breeding techniques to develop new varieties; they use biotechnology to give those varieties an additional desirable characteristic (or beneficial trait) that often cannot be effectively developed through breeding practices alone.

The GM traits we develop typically help farmers increase yields on their farmland, while conserving resources such as soil and water. Examples of these traits are herbicide, insect and drought tolerance. However, we also work to develop traits that can contribute to an improvement in our diets, such as soybeans that produce fatty acids that provide better nutrition.

Are Foods and Ingredients Developed Through Biotechnology (or GMOs) Safe to Eat?

Yes. Plants and crops with GM traits have been tested more than any other crops—with no credible evidence of harm to humans or animals.

There is broad global agreement among food scientists, toxicology experts and regulatory food safety officials on how to evaluate the safety of GM foods.

As consumers ourselves, we place the highest priority on the safety of our products and conduct rigorous and comprehensive testing on each. In fact, seeds with GM traits have been tested more than any other crops in the history of agriculture—with no credible evidence of harm to humans or animals.

Governmental regulatory agencies, scientific organizations and leading health associations worldwide agree that food grown from GM crops is safe to eat. The World Health Organization, the American Medical Association, the U.S. National Academy of Sciences, the British Royal Society, among others that have examined the evidence, all come to the same conclusion: consuming foods containing ingredients derived from GM crops is safe to eat and no riskier than consuming the same foods containing ingredients from crop plants modified by conventional plant improvement techniques (i.e. plant breeding).

Who Makes Sure Biotech Crops Are Safe to Eat and Safe for the Environment?

Independent scientists and the companies that develop biotech crops conduct tests for food, feed and environmental safety. Scientists at regulatory agencies review this data and are responsible for regulating the crops.

Independent scientists at regulatory agencies worldwide review the data for each potential product and make their own scientific assessment of its food, feed and environmental safety. There is broad global agreement among food scientists, toxicology experts and regulatory food safety officials on how to evaluate the safety of GM foods; and this strong regulatory framework has successfully ensured the safety of GM seeds.

Since GM crops were first commercialized in 1996 (1996–2012), regulatory agencies in 59 countries have conducted extensive scientific reviews and affirmed the safety of GM crops with 2,497 approvals on 319 different GMO traits in 25 crops. The majority (1,129) of approvals on GM crops have been on the food safety of the product.

Monsanto makes submissions to regulatory agencies in countries where we plan to sell our seed or where the crop is commonly imported. Regulatory agencies in each country must approve a potential product before it can be sold to farmers, or imported for food and/or animal feed in their country. In the United States, for example, three agencies share responsibility for overseeing and approving GM crops based on their specific areas of scientific expertise:

- The Food and Drug Administration (FDA) is responsible for the safety and appropriate labeling of food and feed products grown from GM crops. This includes a review of nutrient composition, non-nutrient composition and the potential presence of allergens.

- The Department of Agriculture (USDA) is responsible for ensuring that GM crops are safe for agriculture. USDA oversees and regulates field testing, as well as the movement of GM crops and seeds.

- The Environmental Protection Agency (EPA) is responsible for the safety of pesticides, and so is responsible for reviewing GM plants that produce proteins to protect the plants from insect pests and disease. The EPA oversees field testing, as well as the sale and distribution of pest-protected crops to ensure public and environmental health.

Can Consumers Avoid GM Foods in the Grocery Store If Desired?

Yes. Consumers can look for and choose those products that are labeled "certified non-GM product" or "certified organic" products.

GM crops can provide farmers with the means to improve yields under weed and insect pressure; decrease tillage to protect soil and water resources; and reduce pesticide applications.

Are Foods and Ingredients Developed From Genetically Modified (GM) Crops Labeled?

Many countries have different approaches to food labeling, both on GM ingredients and other things. In the United States, all ingredients must be listed, and when there is a meaningful difference in the safety, composition or nutrition of the crop from which they were derived, that difference is properly reflected on the label.

Each country establishes its own food labeling laws. Within the United States, the FDA requires the labeling of ingredients. If there is a *meaningful difference in the safety, composi-*

tion or nutrition of the crop from which the ingredients were derived, the FDA could require additional information be added to the label. This is not the case for GM ingredients. Recently the American Medical Association [AMA] re-affirmed that there is no scientific justification for special labeling of foods that contain GM ingredients; the American Association for the Advancement of Science stated a similar stance. We support these positions and the FDA's approach.

However, we also support a food company's right to voluntarily label its products to highlight or market attributes that are important to its customers, such as products that are certified organic or products labeled as not containing GM ingredients. FDA's labeling laws allow for voluntary labeling as long as the information is accurate, truthful and avoids misleading consumers about the food. We support voluntary labeling and a consumer's right to choose products based on the attributes that meet their individual preferences.

Do GM Crops Provide Any Benefits?

Yes. GM crops can improve yields for farmers, reduce draws on natural resources and fossil fuels and provide nutritional benefits.

As demonstrated by the unprecedentedly rapid adoption of this technology among farmers, GM crops can provide farmers with the means to improve yields under weed and insect pressure; decrease tillage to protect soil and water resources; and reduce pesticide applications, thereby decreasing the use of fossil fuels. Some benefits, such as decreased insecticide applications, also are benefits recognized by consumers and environmentalists.

In addition, some GM crops provide nutritional benefits. For example, certain GM crops produce more nutritious oils (i.e. high oleic soybean oils), which can help people replace solid fat in their diets, potentially reducing saturated fat intake. Another example includes stearidonic acid (SDA)-

containing soybeans, that produce healthful long chain omega-3 fatty acids like EPA.

Has Anyone Studied the Long-Term Health Effects of GM Crops (GMOs)?

Many studies are conducted to assess health effects of GM crops.

Since farmers first began growing biotech crops in 1996, there has been no credible evidence of harm to humans or animals. In addition, the following two studies assessed the long-term safety of GMOs:

- In December 2010, the European Commission published a report summarizing the results of 50 research projects addressing the safety of GMOs for the environment as well as for animal and human health. These projects received funding of €200 million from the EU [European Union] and are part of a 25-year long research effort on GMOs. In announcing the report, the Commission stated, ". . . there is, as of today, no scientific evidence associating GMOs with higher risks for the environment or for food and feed safety than conventional plants."

- In 2012, a literature review of well-designed, long-term and multigenerational animal feeding studies comparing GM and non-GM potatoes, soy, rice, corn and triticale found that GM crops and their non-GM counterparts are nutritionally equivalent and can be safely used in food and feed.

In Addition to Animal Feeding Studies, Are Human Clinical Trials Used to Test the Safety of Biotech (GM) Crops?

There are not currently any human clinical trials used to test the safety of GM crops. This is not unusual; no existing food or ingredient—GM or otherwise—has been the subject of human clinical trials. However, there is broad global agreement among food scientists, toxicology experts and regulatory food safety officials on how to evaluate the safety of GM foods. We follow these expert recommendations.

Experts in the field of food safety ... assure the GM crops are as safe as their conventional counterparts.

The starting point is identifying differences between GM crops and their conventional counterparts. The experts agree that components of GM crops that are the same as existing foods do not require testing. As a result, the focus is on what is different in the GM crop—the inserted DNA/RNA and the proteins resulting from gene insertion.

DNA and RNA are a normal part of every plant and animal, and therefore in virtually every meal we eat. DNA and RNA carry no dietary hazard and are "generally recognized as safe" (GRAS) in the United States, and are considered safe by food safety experts globally. Proteins are also a normal part of the human diet, are extensively digested, and generally present no hazards, but that must be confirmed for the specific proteins introduced in GM crops. To do this, an analysis of protein structure and function is performed and testing of digestibility is conducted to establish safety of the introduced proteins.

As long as the introduced gene protein is determined safe (an initial step in the safety assessment) and the GM and non-GM crops are alike in all respects, the GM crop is said to be substantially equivalent, or "equal to," their conventional counterparts and are not expected to pose any health risks. Experts in the field of food safety are satisfied that this approach is sufficient and reliable to assure the GM crops are as safe as their conventional counterparts. This expert community does not see a need and thus does not recommend long-term tests in humans in order to establish food safety.

Further, it is quite difficult and somewhat impractical to design a long-term safety test in humans. These types of tests using whole foods would require, for example, dietary intake of significantly large amounts of a particular food—amounts not typically consumed—over a very large span of time. This is, in part, why no existing whole foods—whether from organic, conventional or GM production—have been subjected to long-term human clinical trials.

Is Food Grown with or Developed from Biotech Seeds Contributing to Allergies in America?

The process of GM development has safeguards to prevent the introduction of new allergens. There is no evidence of any new allergens being introduced in GM foods.

Like anyone with products connected to food, we take food allergies very seriously. The process of GM development has safeguards to prevent the introduction of new allergens. There is no evidence of any new allergens being introduced in GM foods.

It is important to note that there are hundreds of thousands of different proteins in the human diet, and only a tiny fraction of these are significant food allergens. Thus, the risk of a new protein being a food allergen is very low. Regardless, in the initial stages of product development, Monsanto researchers avoid sources of known allergens, such as nuts and eggs, as potential gene sources for GM crops.

No matter the source of the gene though, we assess every new protein for certain characteristics to help avoid the introduction of potential allergens into a GM crop. Assessing for potential allergenicity of introduced proteins is an FDA-required component of the safety assessment of GM crops.

I've Seen Conflicting Reports on Safety. What Should I Believe?

It's true that there is a lot of conflicting information out there. But when it comes to the scientific community that has studied the issue, there really isn't any conflict—the broad consensus among scientists who have looked closely at GM crops is that they are as safe as any other crop.

When considering and comparing scientific data, there are several things we take into account:

- Is the study designed and executed well and according to accepted methods?

- Is it in alignment with other data on the same topic?

- Do the results make scientific/biological sense?

- Is the scope of the conclusions supported by the data?

- What is the opinion of credible scientific organizations such as regulatory agencies, AMA, National Academy of Sciences?

There is a large body of documented scientific testing showing that the GM crops being grown and harvested are safe (Center for Environmental Risk Assessment). These studies focus on the wholesomeness and nutritional value of GM crops and upon the safety of the specific varieties used.

3

Genetically Modified Foods Are Not Safe to Eat

Joseph Mercola

Joseph Mercola is an osteopath and a 2012 American College of Nutrition fellow; he has authored dozens of scientific papers in addition to the best-selling books, The Great Bird Flu Hoax *and* The No-Grain Diet.

A former biotech research scientist whose job was to reassure the public about the safety of genetically modified (GM) crops has reconsidered his position and is now speaking out strongly against GM foods. Thierry Vrain believes that genetic engineering is based on a flawed understanding of how gene transfer works, and he maintains that serious problems could arise because of it. The widely accepted safety of GM food is based on that faulty gene-transfer hypothesis, and GM foods could pose significant health risks that have not been properly studied. Agribusiness giants like Monsanto Company typically block independent research on their products and rely on positive reports from researchers within the biotech industry for proof that their products are safe. Nothing could be further from the truth; GM foods are dangerous for human health and the environment, and they are unsafe to eat.

Who better to speak the truth about the risks posed by genetically modified (GM) foods than Thierry Vrain, a former research scientist for Agriculture Canada? It was Vrain's job to address public groups and *reassure them* that GM crops and food were safe, a task he did with considerable knowledge and passion.

But Vrain, who once touted GM crops as a technological advancement indicative of sound science and progress, has since started to acknowledge the steady flow of research coming from prestigious labs and published in high-impact journals—research showing that there is significant reason for concern about GM crops—and he has now changed his position.

Genetic engineering is based on an extremely oversimplified model.

Vrain cites the concerning fact that it is studies done by Monsanto and other biotech companies that claim GM crops have no impact on the environment and are safe to eat. But federal departments in charge of food safety in the US and Canada have *not* conducted tests to affirm this alleged "safety."

Vrain writes:

"There are no long-term feeding studies performed in these countries [US and Canada] to demonstrate the claims that engineered corn and soya are safe. All we have are scientific studies out of Europe and Russia, showing that rats fed engineered food die prematurely.

These studies show that proteins produced by engineered plants are different than what they should be. Inserting a gene in a genome using this technology can and does result in damaged proteins. The scientific literature is full of studies showing that engineered corn and soya contain toxic or allergenic proteins.

... I refute the claims of the biotechnology companies that their engineered crops yield more, that they require less pesticide applications, that they have no impact on the environment and of course that they are safe to eat."

Genetic Engineering Technology Is Based on a Misunderstanding

This misunderstanding is the "one gene, one protein" hypothesis from 70 years ago, which stated that each gene codes for a single protein. However, the Human Genome project completed in 2002 failed dramatically to identify one gene for every one protein in the human body, forcing researchers to look to epigenetic factors—namely, "factors beyond the control of the gene"—to explain how organisms are formed, and how they work.

According to Vrain:

"Genetic engineering is 40 years old. It is based on the naive understanding of the genome based on the One Gene–one protein hypothesis of 70 years ago, that each gene codes for a single protein. The Human Genome project completed in 2002 showed that this hypothesis is wrong.

The whole paradigm of the genetic engineering technology is based on a misunderstanding. Every scientist now learns that any gene can give more than one protein and that inserting a gene anywhere in a plant eventually creates rogue proteins. Some of these proteins are obviously allergenic or toxic."

In other words, genetic engineering is based on an extremely oversimplified model that suggests that by taking out or adding one or several genes, you can create a particular effect or result. But this premise, which GMO [genetically modified organism] expert Dr. Philip Bereano calls "the Lego model," is not correct. You cannot simply take out a yellow piece and put in a green piece and call the structure identical because there are complex interactions that are still going to take place and be altered, even if the initial structure still stands.

Serious Problems May Arise from Horizontal Gene Transfer

GE [genetically engineered] plants and animals are created using horizontal gene transfer (also called horizontal inheritance), as contrasted with vertical gene transfer, which is the mechanism in natural reproduction. Vertical gene transfer, or vertical inheritance, is the transmission of genes from the parent generation to offspring via sexual or asexual reproduction, i.e., breeding a male and female from one species.

By contrast, horizontal gene transfer involves injecting a gene from one species into a completely different species, which yields unexpected and often unpredictable results. Proponents of GM crops assume they can apply the principles of vertical inheritance to horizontal inheritance, but according to Dr. David Suzuki, an award-winning geneticist, this assumption is flawed in just about every possible way and is "just lousy science."

Genes don't function in a vacuum—they act in the context of the entire genome. Whole sets of genes are turned on and off in order to arrive at a particular organism, and the entire orchestration is an activated genome. It's a dangerous mistake to assume a gene's traits are expressed properly, regardless of where they're inserted. The safety of genetically modified food is based only on a hypothesis, and this hypothesis is already being proven *wrong*.

Leading Scientists Disprove GMO Safety

Vrain cites the compelling report "GMO Myths and Truths" as just one of many scientific examples disputing the claims of the biotech industry that GM crops yield better and more nutritious food, save on the use of pesticides, have no environmental impact whatsoever and are perfectly safe to eat. The authors took a science-based approach to evaluating the available research, arriving at the conclusion that most of the scientific evidence regarding safety and increased yield potential do *not at all* support the claims. In fact, the evidence demonstrates the claims for genetically modified foods are not just wildly overblown—they simply *aren't true.*

Monsanto CEO Hugh Grant claims genetically engineered crops are "the most-tested food product that the world has ever seen."

The authors of this critical report include Michael Antoniou, PhD, who heads the Gene Expression and Therapy Group at King's College at London School of Medicine in the UK [United Kingdom]. He's a 28-year veteran of genetic engineering technology who has himself invented a number of gene expression biotechnologies; and John Fagan, PhD, a leading authority on food sustainability, biosafety, and GE testing. If you want to get a comprehensive understanding of genetically engineered foods, I strongly recommend reading this report.

Not only are genetically modified (GM) foods less nutritious than non-GM foods, they pose distinct health risks, are inadequately regulated, harm the environment and farmers, and are a poor solution to world hunger. Worse still, these questionable GM crops are now polluting non-GM crops, leading to contamination that cannot ever be "recalled" the way you can take a bad drug off the market ... once traditional foods are contaminated with GM genes, *there is no going back!* Vrain expanded:

> "Genetic pollution is so prevalent in North and South America where GM crops are grown that the fields of conventional and organic grower are regularly contaminated with engineered pollen and losing certification. The canola and flax export market from Canada to Europe (a few hundreds of millions of dollars) were recently lost because of genetic pollution."

Warnings Have Been Ignored

In 2009, the American Academy of Environmental Medicine called for a *moratorium on genetically modified foods*, and said that long-term independent studies must be conducted, stating:

> "Several animal studies indicate serious health risks associated with GM food, including infertility, immune problems, accelerated aging, insulin regulation, and changes in major organs and the gastrointestinal system. . . . There is more than a casual association between GM foods and adverse health effects. There is causation . . ."

Despite this sound warning, GM foods continue to be added to the US food supply with no warning to the Americans buying and eating this food. Genetic manipulation of crops, and more recently food animals, is a dangerous game that has repeatedly revealed that assumptions about how genetic alterations work and the effects they have on animals and humans who consume such foods are deeply flawed and incomplete. Monsanto CEO [chief executive officer] Hugh Grant claims genetically engineered crops are "the most-tested food product that the world has ever seen." What he doesn't tell you is that:

1. Industry-funded research predictably affects the outcome of the trial. This has been verified by dozens of scientific reviews comparing funding with the findings of the study. When industry funds the research, it's virtually guaranteed to be positive. Therefore, independent studies must be done to replicate and thus verify results.

2. The longest industry-funded animal feeding study was 90 days, which recent research has confirmed is FAR too short. In the world's first independently funded lifetime feeding study, massive health problems set in during and after the 13th month, including organ damage and cancer.

3. Companies like Monsanto and Syngenta rarely if ever allow independent researchers access to their patented seeds, citing the legal protection these seeds have under patent laws. Hence independent research is extremely difficult to conduct.

4. There is no safety monitoring. Meaning, once the GM item in question has been approved, not a single country on Earth is actively monitoring and tracking reports of potential health effects.

It Might Take More than One Bite to Kill You . . .

"One argument I hear repeatedly is that nobody has been sick or died after a meal (or a trillion meals since 1996) of GM food," Vrain said. "Nobody gets ill from smoking a pack of cigarettes either. But it sure adds up, and we did not know that in the 1950s before we started our wave of epidemics of cancer. Except this time it is not about a bit of smoke, it's the whole food system that is of concern. The corporate interest must be subordinated to the public interest, and the policy of substantial equivalence must be scrapped as it is clearly untrue."

Unless a food is certified organic, you can assume it contains GMO ingredients if it contains sugar from sugar beets, soy, or corn, or any of their derivatives.

Remember, Vrain used to give talks about the *benefits* of genetically modified foods, but he simply couldn't ignore the research any longer . . . and why, then, should you? All in all, if GM foods have something wrong with them that potentially could cause widespread illness or environmental devastation, Monsanto would rather NOT have you find out about it. Not through independent research, nor through a simple little label that would allow you to opt out of the experiment, should you choose not to take them on their word. As Vrain continued:

> "The Bt corn and soya plants that are now everywhere in our environment are registered as insecticides. But are these insecticidal plants regulated and have their proteins been tested for safety? Not by the federal departments in charge of food safety, not in Canada and not in the U.S.
>
> ... We should all take these studies seriously and demand that government agencies replicate them rather than rely on studies paid for by the biotech companies ... Individuals should be encouraged to make their decisions on food safety based on scientific evidence and personal choice, not on emotion or the personal opinions of others."

At present, the only way to avoid GM foods is to ditch processed foods from your grocery list, and revert back to whole foods grown according to organic standards.

Vote with Your Pocketbook, Every Day

... Voting with your pocketbook, at every meal, matters. It makes a huge difference.

I encourage you to continue educating yourself about genetically engineered foods, and to share what you've learned with family and friends. Remember, unless a food is certified organic, you can assume it contains GMO ingredients if it contains sugar from sugar beets, soy, or corn, or any of their derivatives.

If you buy processed food, opt for products bearing the USDA 100% Organic label, as certified organics do not permit GMO's. You can also print out and use the Non-GMO Shopping Guide, created by the Institute for Responsible Technology. Share it with your friends and family, and post it to your social networks. Alternatively, download their free iPhone application, available in the iTunes store. You can find it by searching for ShopNoGMO in the applications. For more in-depth information, I highly recommend reading the following two books, authored by Jeffrey Smith, the executive director of the Institute for Responsible Technology:

- *Seeds of Deception: Exposing Industry and Government Lies about the Safety of the Genetically Engineered Foods You're Eating,* and

- *Genetic Roulette: The Documented Health Risks of Genetically Engineered Foods.*

For timely updates, join the Non-GMO Project on Facebook, or follow them on Twitter.

Please, do your homework. Together, we have the power to stop the chemical technology industry from destroying our food supply, the future of our children, and the earth as a whole. All we need is about five percent of American shoppers to simply *stop* buying genetically engineered foods, and the food industry would have to reconsider their source of ingredients—regardless of whether the products bear an actual GMO label or not.

4

Genetically Modified Crops Harm the Environment

Center for Food Safety

The Center for Food Safety is a nonprofit public interest and environmental advocacy group that works to protect human health and the environment by curbing the use of harmful food production technologies, and by promoting organic and other forms of sustainable agriculture.

Instead of lessening the contamination of air, water, and soil like biotech companies promised, genetically modified (GM) crops have actually worsened chemical contamination of the environment in several ways. One way is by the spread of GM material to wild species and organic agriculture by accidental cross-pollination, seed mixing, and other unintended means. Another is by creating "superweeds" that develop resistance to the pesticides that GM crops are engineered to withstand. This creates a need to develop new GM crops that are resistant to yet more chemicals that can kill the superweeds. Such a cycle makes the agriculture industry even more dependent on chemicals, and that means more toxic pollution in the air, water, and soil. Biological pollution from GM crops harms the environment and can change whole ecosystems forever.

Despite the misleading claims of companies selling them. Genetically engineered (GE) crops will not alleviate traditional environmental concerns, such as the chemical contamination of water, air or soil. Far from eliminating pesticides, GE crops have actually increased this chemical pollution. Plants engineered to tolerate herbicides closely tie crop production to increased chemical usage. Crops engineered with Bt genetic material to protect against specific insect pests may decrease the efficacy of this important nonchemical pesticide by increasing resistance to it. This could mean the widespread conversion of this sustainable method of farming to chemical-intensive methods.

Meanwhile, genetic engineering has brought an entirely new slate of environmental concerns. Altered genes engineered into commercial plants are escaping into populations of weeds and unaltered crops. Genetically enhanced "superweeds" may well become a severe environmental problem in coming years. Even now, GE corn, canola and, to a lesser extent, soybeans and cotton are contaminating their non-GE counterparts. This is causing major economic concerns among farmers and is resulting in the loss of U.S. agricultural exports. The biological pollution brought by GE crops and other organisms will not dilute or degrade over time. It will reproduce and disseminate, profoundly altering ecosystems and threatening the existence of natural plant varieties and wildlife.

Regulation and Testing Are Lacking

Despite these troubling and unprecedented environmental concerns, the U.S. government has allowed companies to grow and sell numerous gene-altered crops. Yet no government agency has thoroughly tested the impact of these crops on biodiversity or farmland and natural ecosystems. No regulatory structure even exists to ensure that these crops are not causing irreparable environmental harm. The FDA [US Food and Drug Administration] our leading agency on food safety, requires no mandatory environmental or human safety testing of these crops whatsoever. Nonetheless, officials at the FDA,

EPA [US Environmental Protection Agency] and USDA [US Department of Agriculture] have allowed, and even promoted, GE crop plantings for years.

Once biological pollutants enter the environment, the results are irreversible and ecosystems are forever changed.

The lack of government oversight is troubling. Each decision to introduce these biological contaminants into our environment is a dangerous game of ecological roulette. The extent of irreversible environmental damage grows greater with every new acre of GE cropland and every new GE variety.

Biological Pollution

The term "pollution" evokes thoughts of factory smokestacks capped by billowing columns of acrid smoke or lifeless streams foaming with putrid agricultural or industrial runoff. For decades environmentalists have focused on reducing or eliminating these and other forms of chemical pollution. Now, the commercialization of biotechnology has raised concerns among scientists, farmers and the public over a much more subtle yet potentially more insidious form of pollution—the biological contamination of wild species, organic crops and other agricultural products.

Unlike chemical pollutants, biological pollutants reproduce, disseminate and mutate. They do not degrade over time as chemicals do, but rather multiply exponentially. Disastrous U.S. experiences with exotic bio-invaders such as Dutch elm disease, chestnut blight and the kudzu vine attest to the pernicious problem of biological pollution. As demonstrated by these exotics, once biological pollutants enter the environment, the results are irreversible and ecosystems are forever changed.

Plant geneticist Dr. Norman C. Ellstrand describes the difference between chemical and biological pollution: "A single molecule of DDT [pesticide banned in United States in 1972] remains a single molecule or degrades, but a single crop [gene] has the opportunity to multiply itself repeatedly through reproduction, which can frustrate attempts at containment." Even as agricultural biotechnology brings with it an unprecedented increase in potential biological pollution, its current uses are also likely to increase the use of agricultural chemicals.

Superweeds on the Rise

A major biological pollution problem of GE crops is the creation of "superweeds." Almost all of the world's leading food crops have formed hybrids in nature with weedy relatives. Published research confirms varying degrees of gene flow from domesticated crops to weedy wild relatives for varieties of beets, canola, corn, grapes, millet, radishes, rice, squash and sunflowers. Several studies demonstrate that GE plants are likely to share this propensity, and some may have a strong tendency to pass along traits that could create more persistent, more damaging weeds.

Farmers across the country are struggling to deal with ... resistant weeds on over 10 million acres of cropland.

One example of such research is a 2-year trial on plant/ weed hybridization conducted by Dr. Ellstrand and Dr. Paul E. Arriola of the University of California, Riverside. The trial demonstrated substantial hybridization between sorghum and johnsongrass, a noxious weed that plagues various field and orchard crops. Extreme johnsongrass infestation can reduce corn, cotton and soybean yields by nearly half. Arriola and Ellstrand found sorghum/johnsongrass hybrids growing as far as 100 meters from the nearest sorghum crop, and judged these plants to be as hearty as non-hybrid johnsongrass.

Crops engineered to tolerate herbicides are of particular concern. The biotechnology industry has long known of the potential for its crops to create "superweeds." In fact, scientists at Calgene, the company that introduced the first commercial GE crop, were among the earliest to predict this danger. They noted in 1985, "The sexual transfer of genes to weedy species to create a more persistent weed is probably the greatest environmental risk of planting a new variety of crop species." Since that time, field trials and the experiences of commercial growers have borne out their fears. To control herbicide resistant weeds, farmers are now spraying more toxic herbicides (6 to 8 different types in extreme cases), resorting to more soil-eroding tillage operations, and hiring weeding crews to hoe weeds by hand in cotton-growing states. In Illinois, weed scientist Patrick Tranel predicts that waterhemp resistant to as many as four families of herbicide may soon make it impractical to grow soybeans in some Midwestern fields.

Besides hybridizing with weeds, genetically engineered crops themselves can become superweeds. Once again the major concern is herbicide resistant plants. In the late 1990s, canola farmers in Alberta, Canada, began planting three distinct types of GE seeds specifically designed to withstand the application of certain commercial pesticides. One variety exhibited resistance to Monsanto Co.'s Roundup herbicide, another to Aventis LP's Liberty herbicide, and another to Cyanamid's Pursuit and Odyssey herbicides. By early 2000, all of these varieties had cross-pollinated to the extent that farmers were finding triple-resistant canola, exhibiting the resistance traits of all three GE varieties, growing in and around their fields. This resistance means farmers have to rely on older, more toxic herbicides to eradicate weeds and volunteers.

Chemical Dependence

Since 1996, Roundup Ready systems—Herbicide Resistant (HR) crops resistant to glyphosate, the active ingredient in

Monsanto's weed killer Roundup—have been the mainstay of GE crop plantings. Scientists, environmentalists and agricultural experts warned that reliance on the Roundup Ready system would create weeds that would build resistance to the herbicide, based on the same Darwinian principle by which overused antibiotics foster drug-resistant bacteria; that is precisely what has happened. Massive use of glyphosate with Roundup Ready crops has created an epidemic of glyphosate-resistant weeds. Now, farmers across the country are struggling to deal with these resistant weeds on over 10 million acres of cropland.

Eighty-four percent of the GE crops planted today are designed to withstand massive applications of herbicides without dying. HR crops are the chief focus of biotechnology development efforts for 2 basic reasons.

First, all of the major biotech companies are pesticide firms that have acquired seed companies. Biotechnology = pesticides + seeds. Second, herbicides are far and away the most heavily used form of pesticide, comprising two-thirds of agricultural pesticide use in the U.S.

HR crops thus create incredibly profitable synergies for Monsanto, Dow and the other pesticide-seed firms, which profit twice by selling both expensive GE seeds and the large quantities of the herbicide(s) used with them.

Now, in a misguided effort to fix the weed resistance problem created by first generation HR crops, biotechnology companies are racing to genetically engineer new crops resistant to ever more toxic herbicides. For example, Dow Chemical Company is currently requesting USDA approval of a GE version of corn that is resistant to 2,4-D, an ingredient in the highly toxic "Agent Orange" used during the Vietnam war. Commercial approval of Dow's corn would trigger a large increase in 2,4-D use. The chemical arms race with weeds triggered by these HR crops entails an ever-escalating spiral of pesticide use and pollution, and attendant adverse impacts on public health and the environment.

Genetic Contamination

Superweeds are not the only consequence of unwanted gene-flow. Volunteer crops, cross pollination, and poorly segregated seed stocks have led to widespread contamination of non-engineered crops. This is potentially devastating for organic farmers and others wishing to keep their crops free from GE contamination. The pervasiveness of genetic contamination effectively denies farmers and consumers the ability to choose to avoid growing and eating GE crops and foods.

The proliferation of GE varieties has ensured that contamination of non-GE crops, either through cross-pollination or the failure to properly segregate seeds and harvests, is rampant. David Gould, who serves on organic certification committees in California and North Dakota, reported that as early as 2000, virtually all the seed corn in the U.S was contaminated with at least a trace of genetically engineered material, and often more. Even the organic lots are showing traces of biotech varieties. Controlling the spread of GE contamination has proven all but impossible.

The primary strategy for preventing Bt resistance relies on planting refuges—sections of fields growing non-Bt crops in proximity to the Bt varieties.

Beyond Gene Flow

Bacillus thuringiensis (Bt) is a family of bacteria that serves as a natural pesticide, because its various subspecies produce proteins (such as Cry9C) toxic to a variety of crop pests. Typically, Bt degrades quickly and poses few toxicity risks to humans, wildlife, or beneficial insects. Therefore, it has become a favored low-impact pesticide for occasional agricultural use. Because Bt is not a manmade pesticide, it is particularly important to organic farmers. Genetically engineered Bt crops constantly produce an activated form of Bt toxin. A published study on Bt cotton states, "This system amounts to a continuous spraying of an entire plant with the toxin, except for the application is from the inside out." Not surprisingly, concentrations of protein toxins are much higher in the tissues of Bt crops than in sprays that farmers apply topically.

Harm to Non-Target Insects

Crops engineered to produce Bt toxins or other insecticides are likely to affect a variety of insects, including those that are not crop pests. A highly publicized study led by Dr. John E. Losey of Cornell University determined that pollen from Bt corn can dust milkweed leaves near cornfields and reduce the survival rate of monarch butterfly larvae that feed on the milkweed. Some scientists have challenged the so-called "monarch study," arguing that Losey's results in a controlled experiment do not translate to real world settings. Subsequent research, however, suggests that natural dusting of milkweed by Bt corn pollen can indeed reduce the survival of monarch larvae up to 10 meters from the edge of a GE cornfield. A study involving Novartis' Event 176 varieties of Bt corn found that they interfered with the normal development of the non-target black swallowtail. Research into how Bt crops' toxicity to non-target insects affects wider ecosystems is incomplete. For example, it is uncertain whether high levels of Bt produced by GE crops could have a counterproductive effect by killing beneficial insects and parasites that naturally reduce crop pests. One study found that Bt Cry1Ab toxin is harmful to the green lacewing, a beneficial predator that feeds on aphids.

While non-target butterflies and moths affected by Bt corn do not prey on crop pests, they do feed on weedy plants, function as pollinators, and sustain populations of beneficial predators by providing an additional food source. Non-target insects also serve as prey for birds and bats. One study found spraying forests with conventional Bt toxin impacted the food supply of the black-throated blue warbler, resulting in reduced breeding activity by the birds and causing their rate of reproduction to fall below their rate of mortality.

Bt Resistance

Most researchers and farmers consider Bt resistance to be a serious threat. For about 30 years Bt toxin has been applied on the spot . . . and only when there are signs of infestation of the crops by insects. It is the most successful biological insecticide control system we have and would probably retain its potency against pests for many more years to come. The primary strategy for preventing Bt resistance relies on planting refuges—sections of fields growing non-Bt crops in proximity to the Bt varieties. The theory is that pests attacking the refuge crops will mate with those feeding on the Bt crops and prevent resistance from being passed to the next generation. However, it seems unlikely that farmers will maintain sufficient refuge fields close enough to all of their Bt fields to ensure crossbreeding between the various pest populations. We have already begun to see Bt-toxin resistance in those insects that are constantly in contact with these monocultures and feed on them.

The rise of Bt resistance would have an extreme impact on many organic farmers. Without Bt, many of these farmers would suffer greater crop losses or choose more expensive pest-control methods, both of which could increase consumer prices for organic foods. Some organic farmers would undoubtedly turn to chemical pesticides or go out of business, potentially reducing the availability of organic products.

5

Genetically Modified Crops Help Farmers

Andrew Weeks

Andrew Weeks is an award-winning journalist whose work has been published in a variety of newspapers and magazines.

In today's competitive agriculture industry, farmers need all the help they can get. Growing genetically modified (GM) crops is the primary way that farmers can increase their yields and their profits in order to stay competitive. Buying patented GM seeds costs more, but farmers say it is worth it because they can grow significantly more crops per acre than they could with conventional seeds. Using GM seeds also reduces the amount and frequency of herbicides and pesticides that must be applied, which not only brings cost savings but is better for the environment. Future advances in GM technologies, such as the development of drought-resistant plant varieties, could have an even bigger positive impact. Today more than fourteen million farmers in twenty-five countries produce GM crops.

It's a challenging time for farmers: costs are up, technology is constantly changing and competition can be fierce.

Tom Billington, who has been farming since about 1970 in south Twin Falls, ID, said in order for farmers to survive, they must adapt to modern times and its technology.

"How do you stay competitive?" he asked. "You have to use genetic crops, change financially or go out of business."

Billington chose to adapt. Today his crops get a little boost by using genetically modified [GM] seeds, which he said give more bang for the buck. They're more expensive to purchase because they're patented seeds, he said, but the output is better.

He can grow more product—alfalfa and corn—in a season because of GM seeds than he ever did growing organic, which helps him stay competitive in an industry where demand continues to increase.

Sitting at the table in a cafe Thursday [April 25, 2013] eating his lunch, Billington used Sun Chips to make his point.

"Without genetics this is what you have," he said.

A lone chip sat on the table.

"But with genetics you get this."

He placed several other chips around the one.

GM crops, which are grown on most of the farms in southern Idaho, according to Justin Tolley, crop advisor for Crop Production Services in Hansen [Idaho], are disease resistant, insect resistant and take less chemicals to make them green and productive.

His company sells DeKalb seeds—about 10,000 acres of it per season, he said.

"I haven't sold a bag of corn seed that wasn't GM," Tolley said. "99.9 percent of the farmers in southern Idaho grow GM crops."

Corn is the most popular seed he sells, but alfalfa is picking up.

Genetically modified crops aren't new, . . . George Washington started all this when he experimented with his apple orchards in the 1700s.

Thirty tons per acre is a good crop for organic corn, he said. With GM seeds, the output increases to about 35 tons per acre and up to as much as 40 tons.

"We see an increase in production because we limit compaction and don't go over fields so many times with pesticide applications," said Dave Hyde, seed sales and marketing manager for J.R. Simplot. "Nationwide, we're seeing probably a six bushel increase per acre.

"GMOs [genetically modified organisms] grow better in our environment," Hyde said. "We still have to spray, but instead of maybe five times a year, we're doing it once or twice."

The Crops

Genetically modified crops aren't new, Billington said, adding that George Washington started all this when he experimented with his apple orchards in the 1700s.

What is new is technology, increased population and demand.

Today, more than 14 million farmers in 25 countries produce GM crops—an 80-fold increase since 1996, when GM seeds were first commercialized, according to the International Service for the Acquisition of Agri-biotech Applications, a nonprofit that monitors the use of GM crops.

Popular crops that are genetically modified in Idaho include alfalfa, corn and sugarbeets, but there also is research going on with potatoes and wheat. Most of the soybeans in the Midwest are genetically modified.

"Our association supports GMOs because they'd help meet the challenges of production that growers face," said Travis Jones, executive director of the Idaho Grain Producers Association.

Currently, he said, there are no genetically modified barley or wheat crops in the state, but research is under way on creating GM wheat.

"I'm not sure that there is much going on with barley right now," he said. "The biggest industry that uses barley are the beer companies and they're not too excited about GM barley."

There also are no genetically modified potatoes, but that likely will change in the future.

Dave Hyde, seed sales and marketing specialist for J.R. Simplot, said about 98 percent of corn crops in Idaho are genetically modified. Sugarbeet crops are a close second at about 95 percent, he said, and alfalfa crops are at about 20 percent.

Monsanto, based in St. Louis, Mo., is the largest GM research company in the country, making Roundup Ready resistant seeds, but other companies also experiment with seed genetics.

"We've gone in and inserted some enzymes and proteins that make corn resistant to certain pests," Hyde said. "In the past, we've gone in with a blanket pesticide application, but because of GMOs we're able to show what pests we're going after. Therefore, we use less pesticide in the environment. In some production systems we're seeing as much as 80 percent less pesticide in the environment because we're able to rely on GMOs and what they can bring to the table."

The Controversy

Three years ago, Jenny Easley watched a documentary about how food is made. One of the things mentioned in the program was genetically modified foods, and it got her thinking: "How healthy is the food that I eat?"

"Hardly any GM foods on the market [in the United States] are labeled. And yet 62 percent of the countries are labeling their GM foods; even China is labeling."

The more research she did, the more convinced she became that a lot of the food on the market was genetically modified but not labeled as such.

That started Easley and friend Leslie Stoddard on a long trip to lobby for labeling on GM foods. The pair created GMOFree Idaho, which touts health risks of genetically modified foods.

Easley said a bill to label GM foods will be sponsored in the next legislative session by Rep. Mat Erpelding, D-Boise.

"We're behind the times," Stoddard said, "because hardly any GM foods on the market are labeled. And yet 62 percent of the countries are labeling their GM foods; even China is labeling."

Stoddard once suffered from ulcerative colitis, she said, caused by the foods she ate. When she switched to organic, things improved and she felt healthier. . . .

A similar push is being made in Vermont by organic farmer Sen. David Zuckerman, who said confusion comes up because some organic vegetable and fruit farms have expanded into raising animals for meat. The animals often are fed conventional grain, but because they come from farms that are otherwise organic, consumers assume the meat is organic, too.

Separating Fact from Fiction

"In the debate over biotech crops, differentiating fact from fiction is not easy," reads a paper on the economic impact of transgenic crops published in 2010 by the International Food Policy Research Institute in Washington, D.C. "The debate has been confused by the influence of rigid, absolutist views (both supportive of and opposed to biotech crops) about the role of science in society, combined with a general ignorance of science."

Tolley said he believes those who oppose GM crops are those who don't work closely with them. It's a different perspective when you're working the fields all day, he said.

"I'm not afraid to eat anything we grow," Tolley said. "They're easier and safer" because farmers don't have to spray them as frequently with herbicide and insecticides.

Mike Heath, owner of M&M Heath Farms near Buhl [Idaho], grows organic crops but said he's had a difficult time growing corn because of pollen drift from area GMO crops. He agrees with Easley that GM foods should become labeled.

"I think customers ought to have a choice," he said. "If anyone is concerned about the issue [then] they better be buying certified organic foods, because otherwise there are no guarantees."

The Future

Billington is proud of his country and proud to contribute to its food output. He's seen both his businesses grow over the past four decades since he first purchased 4.7 acres in south Twin Falls. Despite controversy by some groups, he's thankful for GMOs and how they've helped him improve business. He believes things will only get better.

He isn't the only one.

"What does the future hold for GMOs?" Hyde asked. Many things are happening with alfalfa, he said, which make it more digestible for cows, and technology continues to improve the potential of seeds.

"Every farmer would love to use zero pesticides on their crops," Hyde said. "As time goes on, we're going to come out with more traits to help us out in the field."

Things he's most excited about are drought-resistance corn crops, which also continue to be improved. Eventually, he said, we might see more varieties of drought-resistant crops.

"That alone could have a huge impact statewide, nationwide and even worldwide because less water would be needed to grow crops," he said. "This has the potential to be the magic wand."

glyphosate but also older and more toxic herbicides—such as dicamba and 2,4-D. Thirteen of 20 crops awaiting clearance by the U.S. Department of Agriculture (USDA) for commercial cultivation and sale are engineered to tolerate herbicides other than or in addition to glyphosate. If these crops are approved and widely used, they will only exacerbate the current problem.

> *In addition to harming neighboring crops, drift and volatilization [from herbicides] may harm vegetation in uncultivated areas near farms, such as fencerows and woodlots.*

The herbicides slated for use together with the next generation of resistant crops raise both environmental and human health concerns. Dicamba and 2,4-D are members of a chemical class known as phenoxy herbicides, which studies have associated with increased rates of certain diseases, including non-Hogkins lymphoma, among farmers and farm workers. These herbicides, especially 2,4-D, are also highly prone to drifting on the wind and to volatilizing—dispersing into the air after application—so that they may settle far from where they are sprayed. And they are highly toxic to broadleaf plants—which include many of the most common fruit and vegetable crops.

Twice As Much Herbicide?

Although 2,4-D and dicamba are already in use, the new herbicide-resistant crops would encourage farmers to apply greater quantities of them (as the history of glyphosate use suggests) and to deploy them differently and more dangerously. . . . Some weed scientists have projected a doubling of herbicide use over the next decade if these crops were widely grown. And because the new crops could withstand herbicides being sprayed directly on them during the growing season, farmers would apply them then rather than only in the spring or fall, as is the dominant practice today. While the pesticide industry has developed new formulations of these herbicides that reportedly reduce volatilization, it is unclear how effective they would be and whether reduced volatilization would be offset by greatly increased use. Thus other crops growing nearby could be susceptible to damage, and as a result the local production of high-value crops such as fruits and vegetables may be discouraged in areas where resistant corn and soybeans are prevalent.

Some farmers may plant 2,4-D- or dicamba-resistant soybeans or cotton (both broadleaf crops) as a defensive measure, after neighbors adopt 2,4-D- and dicamba-resistant crops, in order to prevent damage from herbicide drift or volatilization. Cotton is especially sensitive to phenoxy herbicide damage. This defensive measure would further intensify the use of herbicide-resistant crops and the herbicides they require, thereby increasing the likelihood of resistant weeds.

In addition to harming neighboring crops, drift and volatilization may harm vegetation in uncultivated areas near farms, such as fencerows and woodlots. These habitats are critical to harboring beneficial organisms—pollinators and pest insects' natural enemies, for example—that greatly increase crop productivity.

The companies developing the next generation of herbicide-tolerant crops—including Monsanto and Dow Agrosciences—contend that the use of multiple herbicides will stave off further evolution of resistance and check the advance of currently resistant weeds, because most resistance genes confer immunity to only one type of herbicide. In order to develop resistance to multiple herbicides, the companies argue, a weed typically would have to possess genes for resistance to each individual herbicide—a very rare occurrence.

Potential for Multiple Resistances

But there are several problems with this argument. Farmers growing new crops that have resistance to glyphosate and one other herbicide—such as 2,4-D—would deploy only that one effective herbicide when glyphosate-resistant weeds were present. Because glyphosate-resistant weeds are now so prevalent, this scenario may often be the case. In such a situation, the weeds would have to develop resistance to only the one additional herbicide to escape control. Moreover, weeds *can* develop resistance to multiple herbicides through single genes that detoxify multiple types of chemicals.

So it is not surprising that several weed species that include populations of glyphosate-resistant weeds are already showing resistance to at least one other herbicide, including several of the herbicides slated to be used with the next generation of engineered crops. And if weeds that possess resistance to different herbicides happen to mate, the resulting progeny will be multiple-herbicide-resistant weeds—resistant to all of the herbicides that the parent plants could survive. Regarding waterhemp, for example—a prolific weed of corn and soybean fields in the Corn Belt—there is concern that multiple-herbicide resistance may limit farmers' options to less-effective herbicides.

When small amounts of herbicides are used in the context of biodiverse agroecology-based systems, weeds are much less likely to develop resistance.

Rather than delaying resistance, the use of multiple herbicides would lead to the quicker evolution of weeds that have multiple resistances. Such weeds could be a nightmare scenario for farmers who rely primarily on herbicides, given that no fundamentally new types are in development that might be ready in the foreseeable future.

The Science of Agroecology

Recent studies have shown that herbicide use could be reduced by more than 90 percent—while maintaining or increasing yields and net farmer profits—through practices based on the principles of ecological science that reduce weed numbers and growth. These practices include crop rotation (alternating crops from year to year), the use of cover crops and mulches, judicious tillage, and taking advantage of the weed-suppressive chemicals produced by some crops and crop varieties. Even the use of composted livestock manure and crop residues rather than synthetic fertilizers can help to control some weeds, as these methods generally release nutrients more slowly, which can favor the growth of larger-seeded crops over small-seeded weeds.

These agroecological methods have other important benefits, such as increased soil fertility and water-holding capacity, reduced emissions of water pollutants and global warming gases, and enhancement of habitat for pollinators and other beneficial organisms. And when small amounts of herbicides are used in the context of biodiverse agroecology-based systems, weeds are much less likely to develop resistance because selective pressure is greatly decreased.

Limited Study Results

A series of farm-scale experiments in Iowa demonstrated that the application of agroecological principles provides effective control of major weeds present in the Corn Belt [region of Midwestern United States where corn has been the main crop since the 1850s], including waterhemp. Although glyphosate-resistant weeds per se were not present at the research site, the effective methods developed by this and other research projects should control resistant weeds equally well. This is because glyphosate-resistant weeds are not inherently more aggressive or competitive than their nonresistant counterparts. They are simply harder to control chemically.

Few studies to date have tested agroecological methods directly for controlling glyphosate-resistant weeds, but research in the southeastern United States has shown that thick stands of rye cover crops, when killed and flattened to serve as mulch, greatly reduce the growth of glyphosate-resistant Palmer amaranth. While this research does not demonstrate that herbicides could be completely eliminated, it suggests that agroecology-based practices could greatly reduce their use while maintaining high crop yields and revenues.

The Path Forward

Although agroecology-based practices show great promise for helping farmers control weeds without negative consequences, they have been discouraged by (1) federal farm policies that favor production of the same crops year after year, (2) a research agenda that favors monoculture and is greatly skewed toward herbicide use as the primary weed control measure, and (3) the lack of adequate information and technical support to help farmers change their methods.

To encourage the adoption of agroecology-based weed control practices, the Union of Concerned Scientists recommends the following actions:

- Congress should fund, and the USDA [US Department of Agriculture] should implement, the Conservation Stewardship Program, which provides sustained national support for farmers using sustainable weed control methods; such support should include a bonus payment for resource-conserving crop rotations.

- The USDA should institute new regional programs that encourage farmers to address weed problems through sustainable techniques.

- Congress and the USDA should support organic farmers, and those who want to transition to organic, with research, certification, cost-sharing, and marketing programs. Organic agriculture, which controls weeds by means of approaches such as crop rotation, cover crops, and biodiversity, serves as a "test kitchen" for integrated weed management practices that can be broadly applied in conventional systems.

- The USDA should support multidisciplinary research on integrated weed management strategies and should educate farmers in their use.

- The USDA should bring together scientists, industry, farmers, and public interest groups to formulate plans for preventing or containing the development of herbicide-resistant weeds, and the agency should make the approval of new herbicide-tolerant crop varieties conditional on the implementation of such plans.

- The USDA should fund and carry out long-term research to breed crop varieties and cover crops that compete with and control weeds more effectively.

7

Genetically Modified Salmon Could Harm Humans and the Environment

Food & Water Watch

Food & Water Watch is an international nonprofit organization that works to ensure that food, water, and fish are safe, accessible, and sustainably produced.

Designed to grow twice as fast as a normal fish, a genetically engineered (GE) salmon is likely to be the first transgenic animal introduced into the American food supply, pending approval by the US Food and Drug Administration (FDA). Unfortunately, the FDA is not competently assessing the risk of such a move. No long-term studies have been required to evaluate the human health risks associated with eating transgenic fish, even though researchers have documented the ability of other GE foods to harm human health. Of equal concern is the potential impact of GE salmon escaping their farm facilities; they could wipe out wild salmon populations by spreading disease, interfering with breeding, or outcompeting them for food. The FDA is doing a woefully inadequate job investigating the harm GE salmon could cause to both humans and the environment.

The Food and Drug Administration is about to decide whether to unleash genetically engineered (GE) salmon into our food supply. This GE salmon, which is designed to grow twice as fast as normal salmon, would be the first "transgenic" animal allowed into the U.S. food supply. But given how hard the biotechnology industry is pushing genetic manipulation for the animals we eat, it's likely not the last. According to the rhetoric of the salmon's creator, a company called AquaBounty Technologies, this new fish is a technological solution for reducing fishing pressure on wild salmon, creating jobs and diminishing the carbon footprint of producing seafood. But a review of scientific literature tells a far different story, one full of downsides for the consumer, the environment and fishing economies throughout the world.

The commercialization of GE salmon could threaten public health, wipe out wild salmon populations, diminish biodiversity of marine environments, and further drive the unhealthy trend of producing more of the fish we eat in overcrowded, unhealthy factory fish farms.

That's all on top of potentially changing the quality of salmon, one of most popular fish in the U.S. diet.

Unfortunately, the Food and Drug Administration (FDA) appears to have put AquaBounty's salmon in the final stretch of the approval process to become the first GE animal to reach U.S. consumers' tables.

Long-term studies on the safety of eating transgenic organisms have not been conducted, though scientists recognize and have already documented the ability of genetically engineered organisms to harm human and animal health.

To make matters worse, the agency is likely to follow its previous policy on other GE foods and allow this fish to be sold without labeling, leaving consumers without a way to make an informed choice about the food we eat.

The FDA is considering other proposals to commercialize genetically modified animals for use in agriculture, like the

Enviropig, a GE pig designed for use on environmentally damaging factory farms. Biotech corporations' increasing control of the genetic content of our food already has had a massive impact on crops like corn and soybeans, an irresponsible experiment with agricultural production and human health that doesn't need an encore performance with animal agriculture. Unfortunately, the FDA is evaluating GE animals under a process used to approve new animal drugs, which allows the agency to make very little information publicly available until the decision has been made.

AquaBounty Technologies' GE Atlantic salmon reportedly grows to market size in half the time of normal salmon by virtue of the genes implanted into it from other fish. It is unclear if the GE salmon could live up to its rapid-growth hype in large-scale commercial production (many other GE products that were promoted as having dramatically increased crop yields have failed to live up to these claims when used on farms). What is clear is that GE salmon poses risks to the environment and consumer.

GE Salmon's Impact on Human Health

Beyond the enormous damage that GE salmon could cause to the environment and fishing economies, it also poses a risk to human health. Long-term studies on the safety of eating transgenic organisms have not been conducted, though scientists recognize and have already documented the ability of genetically engineered organisms to harm human and animal health.

A *New England Journal of Medicine* study found that soybeans engineered with Brazil nut proteins caused allergic reactions for consumers with Brazil nut allergies. In another case, a harmless protein found in certain beans, which acts as a pest deterrent, became dangerous once it was transferred to a pea, causing allergy-related lung damage and skin problems in mice. One study showed high rat pup mortality in litters from mothers fed GE soy flour. Another found irregularities in the livers of rats, suggesting higher metabolic rates resulting from a GE diet. A 2007 study found significant liver and kidney impairment in rats fed GE corn with the insecticidal *Bt* gene and concluded, "with the present data it cannot be concluded that GE corn MON863 is a safe product." Even GE livestock feed may have some impact on consumers of animal products. Italian researchers found biotech genes in the milk from dairy cows fed a GE diet, suggesting transgenes' ability to survive pasteurization.

Long-term studies have yet to be conducted to assess human health risks associated with eating transgenic fish, yet another indication of the weak process used to evaluate this technology.

To date, the FDA has not done anything to clear up these questions. Critical studies used by the FDA in its analysis of the food safety of GE salmon were conducted by AquaBounty or its contractors. The FDA even says in its analysis, "Primary deference was given to controlled studies submitted by ABT [AquaBounty Technologies]." This is not good enough when the stakes are so high, especially since the studies did show that GE salmon displayed some statistically significant differences in its composition and nutrition.

GE Salmon's Impact on Wild Fish

AquaBounty intends to sell GE salmon eggs to commercial farms to grow out to full size, claiming that these operators will raise fish in contained aquaculture facilities that limit the possibility of escape. The potential impact from escaping GE salmon could be severe, with researchers suggesting that a small number of GE fish escapees could cause extinction of wild populations in as little as 40 generations. Because of their competitive advantage as big, voracious fish, GE salmon could out-compete other wild fish for food and habitat. But the catch is that their own weak constitutions—not designed for the rigors of life outside of captivity—mean that the GE salmon may only last long enough in the wild to prevent natural populations from reproducing, leading to a total extinction of salmon in open waters.

AquaBounty's promises to prevent escapes seem especially weak given the widespread problem of regular farmed salmon escapes from existing farms. In March of 2010, nearly 100,000 farmed Atlantic salmon escaped into the wild through one hole in a net at a UK [United Kingdom] fish farm. Globally, these numbers are much higher, with an estimated 2 million farmed salmon escaping into North Atlantic waters every year while millions of others escape into the Pacific. One biotech corporation doing experimental GE breeding in New Zealand is even suspected of accidentally releasing genetically modified salmon eggs into the wild, demonstrating the logistical difficulties of preventing escapes, even in tightly controlled, experimental settings. AquaBounty, in the environmental assessment it submitted to the FDA, acknowledges, "No single containment measure can be assured of 100% effectiveness."

> *Several studies suggest that an invasion of transgenic fish into a natural fish population could eventually lead to the extinction of both wild and transgenic fish in that region.*

Elsewhere in GE food production, such as with soybeans and corn, industry promises have failed to keep control of genetically engineered traits, causing enormous disruptions in international food markets. The U.S. Government Accountability Office found six known unauthorized releases of GE crops from the United States by 2008. As just one example, in August 2006, the U.S. Department of Agriculture admitted that unapproved GE rice had been found in non-GE rice stocks. Japan immediately halted all U.S. rice imports and Europe imposed heavy restrictions; in total, the event cost the U.S. rice industry $1.2 billion. Biotechnology corporations do not have a track record of responsible ownership and control of their genetic traits, and in the case of GE salmon, this could be particularly damaging, not only to wild fish populations, but to the entire fishing industry.

Competitive Advantage

Because AquaBounty's GE salmon is genetically designed to eat more and grow faster, its escape into the wild would mean the introduction of significant new competitive pressure on wild populations for food and space, as these large, voracious transgenic salmon attempt to quell their hunger by eating more and more.

Currently, non-GE farmed salmon are naturally bred for faster growth, which often means bigger appetites. Once they escape in the wild, they exhibit greater aggression and risk-taking than wild species. This competitive pressure would likely increase with GE salmon, which reportedly grow twice as fast as other salmon.

In addition to out-competing their wild cousins for food and space, GE salmon could interfere with breeding in a variety of ways, pushing wild stocks toward extinction. Added competitive pressure from GE fish can increase stress levels and increase mortality among the wild population, diminishing their ability to effectively breed. In fact, several studies suggest that an invasion of transgenic fish into a natural fish population could eventually lead to the extinction of both wild and transgenic fish in that region.

AquaBounty claims that it will test each commercial batch of eggs it produces to ensure their sterility; however, this batch testing only needs to show a higher than 95 percent sterility rate, meaning that the company may be producing some fertile fish. Additionally, the FDA has called AquaBounty's claim to raise only sterile fish "potentially misleading" because up to 5 percent of eggs sold for grow-out could be fertile. AquaBounty's assurances hardly seem sufficient given the severe consequences that even a small number of fertile GE salmon could have on wild populations.

An additional concern about escaping GE salmon is the disease they could spread to wild populations. Farmed salmon, which are raised in stressful, densely crowded environments, have already been linked to the spread of disease. Infectious hematopoictic necrosis, sea lice and furunculosis disease are three serious ailments that are believed to have been spread by farmed salmon into wild populations. Adding larger, possibly more aggressive GE salmon to this system adds another way to spread the diseases found on factory fish farms to wild fish populations.

Do GE Salmon Still Want to Swim Upstream?

AquaBounty claims that their GE salmon will be "reared in physically contained facilities . . . mitigating any potential risk of a negative impact on genetic diversity of wild stocks." It is unclear how, or if, AquaBounty or the FDA will dictate to aquaculture companies how they must raise the GE salmon. The dominant method of raising salmon is in open net pens in the ocean, which have led to millions of salmon escaping.

AquaBounty has publicly noted the great interest it has received from salmon growers in China, Southeast Asia and Chile, where regulations and oversight on aquaculture are notoriously weak. Given the large number of operators worldwide that would likely use GE salmon eggs (AquaBounty at one point boasted it had orders for 15 million eggs), it seems inconceivable to think that GE salmon won't end up in open-net production or other models where escape is almost guaranteed.

Even closed facilities face myriad challenges in containing farmed fish. In the FDA's review of AquaBounty's environmental assessment, it noted that the company gave scant attention to the potential for natural disaster at its farm facilities in Panama, which are located next to a river that has experienced flooding in recent years.

These gaps in the safety assessment for GE salmon are crucially important because a single GE-salmon escape event—involving only a few fish—can decimate wild populations.

Because AquaBounty will own the intellectual property rights to GE salmon, a decline in wild stocks would boost its market share.

In the mid-1990s, AquaBounty's research manager authored a risk assessment that included a hypothetical scenario involving the commercial production of GE salmon that involved what it called the "usual number of fish escaping." AquaBounty projected that the GE salmon escape would have no negative impact on wild salmon populations, but theorized that the industry would have a beneficial effect on employment by giving Aboriginal Canadians work as fishing guides for the trophy-sized salmon. This cavalier approach to risk assessment seems totally out of synch with the well-documented dangers associated with GE fish, and regulators should take heed.

GE Salmon's Impact on Our Food System

A disconcerting irony of GE salmon is that the worst case scenario for the environment and consumers—wild stocks going extinct because of an accidental release of GE stock—could be the best case scenario for AquaBounty. Because AquaBounty will own the intellectual property rights to GE salmon, a decline in wild stocks would boost its market share, spurring the company to increase production to make up for lost wild fish. For consumers this would mean fewer choices and more GE salmon.

Other markets where GE products have been introduced have experienced this effect, with enormous concentration of power. In 2009, nearly all (93 percent) soybeans and four-fifths (80 percent) of corn cultivated in the United States were grown from seeds containing traits covered by Monsanto patents.

A reduction in wild stocks due to escapes of GE salmon would hurt the fishing industry and could serve to consolidate fish production in corporate-owned fish farms. The fishing industry could suffer, too, if exports of American wild and farmed, non-GE salmon became contaminated with GE traits. American rice and corn farmers have witnessed huge economic losses from the inadvertent intermingling of GE crops and non-GE crops destined for foreign markets in countries with stricter rules on GE food.

AquaBounty has proposed growing its GE salmon eggs in Canada, then shipping them to grow-out facilities in Panama where fish would be raised and processed before shipping them to the United States for sale. With this arrangement, foreign producers, which may not operate under the same regulatory guidelines as in the United States, would be the producers of this controversial new product.

Little Information, Lots of Secrets

AquaBounty posted zero sales and almost 5 million dollars in net losses in 2009; the entire company appears to be wrapped up in the prospects of GE fish for aquaculture. Getting FDA approval is a do-or-die situation for AquaBounty—not a great environment for doing a rigorous and impartial analysis of the risks posed by this new technology.

Unfortunately for consumers, the FDA's guidelines for reviewing GE salmon fail to adequately protect consumers. The FDA does not require a full examination of risks and unintended consequences, including mandatory pre-market safety testing, full pre-market environmental review of all impacts, or public disclosure of the studies and data considered in agency decision-making.

The FDA currently is not assessing GE salmon as a human food product, but rather reviewing the proposal for GE fish as though it were a new animal drug. Clearly, this is an inadequate risk-assessment procedure.

Above all, FDA's process lacks transparency. Existing federal regulations do not require the agency to release important details regarding AquaBounty's GE salmon as part of the new animal drug approval process; therefore little information is available for public review. Given the grave impact that GE salmon may have on the environment and human health—and the impact it may have as a precedent for other GE animals entering the food supply—the FDA's risk-assessment approach to GE salmon is wholly inadequate and leaves consumers at great risk.

8

Genetically Modified Salmon Can Feed the World

Yonathan Zohar

Yonathan Zohar is professor of marine biology and chairman of the Department of Marine Biotechnology at the University of Maryland; he is also interim director of the University of Maryland Institute of Marine and Environmental Technology.

To feed a growing world population, wild global fisheries are being steadily depleted by overfishing and may collapse by midcentury unless significant changes are made. The aquaculture industry has the potential to reverse this trend. Raising the majority of our fish in farms, like other animal and plant crops, would provide the world with an important protein source while conserving natural resources. Since the genetically modified salmon from AquaBounty Technologies grows faster than regular salmon, it is especially well suited for farming, but safeguards are needed to ensure the fish remain securely contained. That concern aside, GM salmon is safe to eat and society should accept the help of science to address the world's "dire need [for] more plentiful and healthier food."

The debate over genetically engineered salmon should be put in the proper context: As the world's population grows at an accelerating pace, so does the consumption of seafood.

This is true not only because there are more mouths to feed, but also because as people become more aware of the health benefits associated with eating seafood, more are switching from meat to fish. To satisfy this demand, we have become very sophisticated fishers, with ever-growing fleets, factory fishing ships and very effective gear.

We efficiently hunt our own seafood in the wild; it seems natural to all of us, while we do not hunt for wild chicken, beef or pork. But fish is harvested at a rate that exceeds the fisheries' ability to replenish themselves.

According to the UN [United Nations] Food and Agricultural Organization, more than 50 percent of the world's main fisheries stocks are fully exploited, while another 28 percent are over-exploited or depleted.

Fish species that used to be plentiful, such as cod, plaice, haddock and others, are now rare in the wild. The king of the oceans, the giant bluefin tuna, is now near the point of no return, its stocks dropping precipitously in the past decade alone.

Reflecting upon these declines, the U.S. has become the world's second largest importer of seafood (after Japan) with more than 80 percent of the seafood consumed in this country coming from overseas. And seafood imports contribute $9 billion annually to the U.S. trade deficit, largest among all agricultural products.

Fisheries scientists have repeatedly warned us that if we do not change our commercial fisheries practices, we will run out of the vast majority of the commercial species by the middle of this century.

This must stop. Like any other animal or plant crop, fish and seafood must be produced through farming—or aquaculture—and the wild stocks should be protected so they can recover. As a society, we must accept that while it is nice to eat wild salmon, there is no wild Atlantic salmon out there; we must get used to eating farmed fish.

Aquaculture Makes Better Fish

The aquaculture industry faces a huge challenge. It must grow fish in a way that is economically viable and environmentally responsible. And this is where genetic engineering enters the picture. Genetically engineered fish, like the AquAdvantage salmon, offer great benefits to fish farmers and should be available to the industry.

We have all been eating selectively bred fish, chicken, beef and other animals for many years without thinking twice about it.

If used carefully, genetic engineering can produce fish that reach the market much faster, as in the AquAdvantage salmon, and use less feed (and thus less fish meal).

As the science develops, it could generate fish that are resistant to disease (currently the aquaculture industry loses billions of dollars annually to disease in its fish population) and healthier for the consumer—making beneficial omega-3 oils available in fish that do not normally contain them, for example.

The public should not be scared by the term "genetic engineering." This powerful platform requires making only relatively minor and very targeted modifications to the animal genome, compared, for example, with selective breeding and domestication, where we manipulate many genes over generations without knowing exactly what is altered.

We have all been eating selectively bred fish, chicken, beef and other animals for many years without thinking twice about it. The AquAdvantage Atlantic salmon has only one extra copy of a fish gene inserted into its genome. This one addition, while enhancing the hormones of the growth axis in fish, operates within the fish's physiological range. And these are fish hormones that have no effect on the human consumer.

Farming Systems Must Be Escape Proof

The AquAdvantage salmon is no different from conventional farmed salmon in its composition and health benefits, and the Food and Drug Administration [FDA] has concluded that it is safe for people to eat.

The single most important caution I would offer is that we must ensure that these fish, as well as any other farmed but domesticated fish (non-genetically engineered), cannot escape from the farming systems to our seas or rivers.

The AquAdvantage salmon must be fully contained, both biologically and physically. Indeed, AquAdvantage salmon are sterile fish, and therefore unable to reproduce even if they escape. These fish are intended to be farmed only in fully contained, land-based farming systems. Every new operation that would grow these fish for sale in the United States would be subject to FDA approval, according to the FDA.

By using multiple and redundant mechanical means to prevent escape (such as screens and filters), as well as reusing the culture water, the systems should be close to full containment, having minimal interactions with the environment. And the implementation of these new, land-based and fully contained marine aquaculture systems offers an opportunity for aquaculture to become more efficient and environmentally sustainable.

However, before approving the genetically engineered fish for use in aquaculture, as a scientist, I would like to see the FDA and AquaBounty be less presumptive and more experimental about the potential environmental risk of AquAdvantage salmon.

Safeguards Are Needed

I want to see scientific data, proof beyond a shadow of a doubt, that if fish do escape from containment, they will not survive, will not breed and will be purged from the environment. Experiments to demonstrate this are all feasible, but will take a few more years to complete.

And finally, consumers should absolutely be informed whether the salmon they are buying is genetically engineered or not. It is our responsibility to make sure the public is educated so the fear factor dissipates and the consumer can make rational decisions regarding genetically engineered salmon. Not labeling the fish will harm the industry altogether as people who do not want genetically engineered fish will avoid farmed salmon altogether.

As a society that is in dire need of more plentiful and healthier food, we must accept the practices of modern agriculture in fish farming. We must trust the power and virtue of the advanced sciences and technology in providing new generations with high-quality food.

We must stop depleting the wild stocks, reducing our biodiversity and harming the oceans around us. Sustainable aquaculture, based on responsible modern biology, including genetic engineering, will provide the world with the seafood that we need and help conserve our planet.

9

Genetically Modified Foods Should Be Labeled

Gary Hirshberg

Gary Hirshberg is the chairman of Just Label It, a grassroots consumer campaign to require the labeling of foods that contain genetically modified ingredients.

Sixty-four countries, including all of the European Union, Russia, and China, require foods containing genetically modified (GM) ingredients to be labeled, but the United States has no such requirement. Because GM foods are so new, there simply isn't enough information to know what the long-term health effects of consuming them might be; and because GM foods are not labeled, health problems cannot be traced back to specific GM ingredients for further study. Food that is genetically modified has been fundamentally altered by that process and the federal government should require labeling on that basis, even if it believes the food to be safe. People have the right to know what they are putting in their bodies, and research shows that 92 percent of the American public wants to know whether the food they eat contains GM organisms.

I am often asked about why GE [genetically engineered] ingredients should be present on our food labels, as well as whether the government actually has the power and responsibility to label.

In a recent presentation at TEDxManhattan [conference], I tried to address these questions, and have highlighted many of them here.

GE plants or animals have had their genetic makeup altered to exhibit traits that are not *naturally* theirs.

In other words, these are organisms created by the transfer and introduction of genetic material from other species in ways that could not occur in nature or through traditional breeding methods. [Agricultural biotechnology company] Monsanto is one of the leading firms in this space. Their website draws a clear distinction between genetically engineered and conventionally bred crops.

Interestingly, the U.S. Commerce Department and specifically the U.S. Patent Office clearly sees these organisms as something unique and new, for they have granted the seed-chemical companies hundreds of patents for these new life forms. And these companies have spent many millions of dollars vigorously and successfully defending their patents from infringement.

Yet over at the U.S. Food and Drug Administration (FDA), there is general presumption that these foods are essentially the same as non-GE foods. In fact, the policy at FDA is that as long as GE crops are "substantially equivalent" to non-GE crops in terms of nutritional parameters like calories, carbohydrates, fiber, and protein, they are also presumably safe, and therefore do not necessitate labels to make consumers aware of when they are buying and eating these foods.

How Common Are GE Foods?

Since 1996, when the first GE crops were approved for commercial use and introduction, they have been extraordinarily successful in penetrating the marketplace. Today, GE soy makes up 90%-plus of the soybeans grown in the US, GE corn is roughly 85% of all corn, and several other GE crops including sugar beets and cotton are equally dominant in the market place.

Particularly because of their dominance in soy and corn, this means that over 70% of the processed foods we eat contain genetically engineered material. The data is clear that the vast majority of Americans do not know that.

We don't yet know, and we probably won't know for a generation, about the impacts of today's first-generation-GE crops.

It is worth noting that 64 other nations around the world including all of the EU [European Union], Russia and China have required labeling when approving these crops.

Because it has only been 16 years since the introduction of GE crops and they have been grown particularly fast in only the last 8 years, we don't yet know, and we probably won't know for a generation, about the impacts of today's first-generation-GE crops. In short, no one can credibly claim whether they are or aren't safe from a long-term perspective. However, there are some bases for concern.

During the 1990's many of the FDA's own scientists warned that genetic engineering was different than traditional breeding and posed special risks of introducing new toxins or allergens, but these warnings were not heeded. Since that time, several National Academy of Sciences studies have affirmed that genetically engineered crops have the potential to introduce new toxins or allergens into our food and environment. Yet unlike the strict safety evaluations for approval of new drugs, there are no mandatory human clinical trials of genetically engineered crops, no tests for carcinogenicity or harm to fetuses, no long-term testing for neurological health risks, no requirement for long-term testing on animals, and limited assessment of the potential to trigger new food allergies.

Companies Are Policing Themselves

There is also growing concern about the lack of independent testing by scientists not funded nor influenced by the companies who own these new patented organisms. Our government's approval of these crops has been based almost exclusively on studies conducted or funded by the chemical companies who own these patented crops to prove that GE food is "substantially equivalent" to its non-GE counterpart.

This is especially troubling because many of the original claims by these companies that led to their approval have subsequently turned out to be false.

One of the very first genetically engineered crops allowed into the commercial market for human consumption was corn and it came with an assurance regarding the insecticide built into its DNA. Chemical companies said the insecticide would not survive more than a few seconds in the human GI tract, and that it would be broken down in saliva. However, a study published two years ago revealed that the insecticide was detected in the umbilical-cord blood of pregnant women.

Because GMOs [genetically modified organisms] are not labeled in the U.S., they might be causing acute or chronic effects, but scientists would have a very hard time recognizing the linkages between GE food intake and unexplained problems. Studying GE food–human health linkages without labeling is like searching for a needle in a haystack with gloves on. . . .

Labels Reflect Changes to Food, Not Safety

While safety is an important question, it is actually not the reason these ingredients and foods need to be labeled. Virtually all of the food and ingredient labeling we see today have no relation to food safety.

If an ingredient poses a food safety hazard, we don't label its presence. We ban it from our food. When the FDA determines that labeling is required for additives like food colorings, dyes or various byproducts, it is not because they have found they are unsafe. The FDA's most important food statute, the Federal Food, Drug and Cosmetic Act, establishes that the consumer has a right to know when something is added to food that changes it in ways a consumer would likely not recognize, and thus labeling is required.

For example, the FDA did not require labeling of irradiated foods because they were hazardous. Rather they found that the process of irradiation caused concern to consumers. So they decided that they should be labeled. The same determination was made with Orange Juice from Concentrate, Country of Origin, Wild vs. Farmed, and many other mandatory components of food labels. Simply put, the FDA found that these processes were relevant and therefore material to the consumer.

Since GE crops look and smell similar and possess similar nutritional qualities [to non-genetically engineered ingredients], they were found to be not "material" to the consumer.

So, I am not saying GMOs should be labeled because they are a proven health risk, rather it is because they add bacterial genes, proteins, and gene fragments never before seen in foods. And we simply don't yet have enough data or experience to know what are the long term impacts of these unprecedented changes to our foods.

Does the FDA Have the Authority to Require Labeling?

The determination that GE crops are "substantially equivalent" to their conventionally grown or bred counterparts is a completely voluntary and discretionary 20-year old internal guideline. This guideline did not result from criteria set forth in legislation passed by Congress to address the unique food safety issues associated with GE foods. Rather these guidelines were recommended by the President's Council on Competitiveness, a panel comprised of government bureaucrats and chemical industry giants under the leadership of VP Dan Quayle in 1992, just a few years before the first GE crops were approved for commercial use.

Putting it simply, the Quayle-led Commission recommended that an ingredient would be deemed "material" for labeling if it possessed nutritional or organoleptic (taste, smell, etc.) differences from their conventional counterparts. And since GE crops look and smell similar and possess similar nutritional qualities, they were found to be not "material" to the consumer.

These guidelines have remained in place for over 20 years, despite countless changes in the US food system and the enormous proliferation of GE crops beyond what anyone expected back in 1992.

The FDA voluntarily adopted these guidelines back then. They have the precedent and the authority to modify those guidelines today.

As someone who has spent my entire adult life advocating for reduced use of toxic chemicals in our foods, agriculture and environment, I am deeply concerned about the proliferation of herbicides and pesticides resulting from GE crop development and the increased resistance that we are seeing with weeds and insects due to their overuse. Consider these three arguments:

Skyrocketing Herbicide Use

Despite assurances to Congress and regulators over the last two decades that crops engineered to be herbicide resistant would lead to less chemical usage, a peer-reviewed paper published last summer [2012] showed that the three major GE crops in the U.S.—corn, soybeans, and cotton—have increased overall herbicide use by more than 527 million pounds between 1996 and 2011, compared to what it likely would have been in the absence of GE crops. The U.S. Geological Survey has reported that glyphosate [Monsanto's Roundup brand weed killer] is now a common component of the air and rain in the Midwest during spring and summer, with levels rising in many aquatic ecosystems.

It's important to note that increased herbicide is just the beginning of the problem.

At least 23 species of weeds are now resistant to glyphosate. Called "superweeds," they are emerging at an alarming rate, and are present in 50–75 million acres where GE soy, corn, and cotton crops grow in 26 states. Several chemical companies are responding by designing GE seeds that tolerate multiple herbicides.

One of the industry's most common arguments is the promise of higher yields from GE crops . . . Yet field trials of soybeans found a 50 percent drop in the yield of GE varieties because of gene disruption.

To combat these resistant weeds, companies are seeking approval of GE crops that are resistant to higher-risk herbicides, such as 2,4-D and Dicamba. Many university weed scientists are speaking out against the dangerous notion that the best way to combat resistant weeds is to spray more herbicides on them—especially herbicides with a proven, negative environmental and human health track record.

And while insecticide use, specifically to prevent corn and cotton insects, actually dropped by 123 million pounds in this same time period, an alarming paper came out in the fall showing that corn borers are now becoming resistant to one of the BT insecticides that was bred into corn since 1996. We, and the biotech industry, continue to ignore this bitter lesson—when farmers press their luck by over-reliance on any single pest control tactic or chemical, resistance is usually just a few years down the road.

So, GE crops have been primarily engineered not for any increased nutritional value or consumer benefit, but to make it easier to control certain insects and spray herbicides on growing crops, killing weeds but leaving the genetically transformed crops unharmed. The technology is a real moneymaker for the industry, which charges much more for the GE seeds, and then sells more herbicide to the farmers planting the seeds.

Patent Holders Are Making False Claims

As mentioned above, despite the industry's claims that herbicide resistant crops would lead to less chemical usage, the opposite has happened. Herbicide use has increased 11% in the past sixteen years.

Corn, one of the first genetically engineered crops, came with an assurance regarding the insecticide built into its DNA. Chemical companies said the insecticide would not survive more than a few seconds in the human GI tract, and that it would be broken down in saliva. However, a study published two years ago revealed that the insecticide was detected in the umbilical-cord blood of pregnant women.

One of the industry's most common arguments is the promise of higher yields from GE crops, which could aid in solving the world's food shortages. Yet field trials of soybeans found a 50 percent drop in the yield of GE varieties because of gene disruption. And hybrid corn varieties engineered with the Bt bacterium to produce a pest-killing protein were slower to develop and ultimately had a 12 percent lower yield than non-GE varieties.

All of these are cases in which the patent holders' claims have not held up. At what point, and at what cost, will we learn to ignore these empty promises, and rely instead on adequate environmental and health assessments?

Lack of Independent Testing

When it comes to the safety of today's first-generation GE crops, we don't yet know, and we probably won't know their impact for a generation. But the concern over the lack of independent testing by scientists not funded nor influenced by the patent holders is growing. Our government's approval of these crops has been based almost exclusively on studies conducted or funded by the chemical companies who own these patented crops to prove that GE food is "substantially equivalent" to its non-GE counterpart.

Many more GE crops are in the approval pipeline. And some of them may very well turn out to offer yield or nutritional benefits, like soybeans with higher levels of heart-healthy omega 3 fatty acids. But for now, while the technology is so young and there is apparently so much to learn, consumers need to have the same rights held by citizens around the world, to choose whether or not to buy these foods and indirectly support this cycle of increased overall chemical usage.

In 2010, the President's Cancer Panel reported that 41% of Americans would be diagnosed with cancer in our lifetimes. The primary culprit that this prestigious panel of senior oncologists identified was the inadvertent daily exposure to numerous chemicals in our air, water and foods. Later that same summer, the journal *Pediatrics* reported a direct correlation between pesticide usage and increased ADHD [Attention Deficit Hyperactivity Disorder] diagnoses.

No one can now definitively prove that the genetic engineering of foods does or does not pose a health or safety threat to any of us. But there is no question that the use of today's GE crops is increasing our exposure to herbicides and BT toxins. I believe that this is highly material to the average consumer.

A Breach of Responsibility

Our government's failure to require labeling, and to be engaged in developing the science supporting GE food risk assessment is an absolute breach of its responsibility to the American public.

There are in fact lots of reasons to label these foods: health and environmental concerns, ethical/religious views or just because people want to know. In fact, Mellman research shows 92% of citizens want the right to know with no meaningful statistical difference between men and women, Republicans and Democrats, urban and rural communities, education level or any demographic.

The bottom line is: without labeling, consumers are completely in the dark. The FDA can label GE foods. And the vast majority of consumers want them to be labeled.

As I always say, this is more than a fight for federal labeling. It is a question of whether our government is of, for and by the people, or of, for and by a handful of chemical companies.

10

Genetically Modified Foods Have Not Been Sufficiently Tested

Ari LeVaux

Ari LeVaux writes "Flash in the Pan," a syndicated weekly food column that has appeared in more than fifty newspapers in twenty-one states. "Flash in the Pan" also regularly appears in TheAtlantic.com, Alternet, Slate, Civil Eats, and other websites and online publications.

Companies that genetically modify food products, such as Monsanto, consistently maintain there is no reason to test the safety of genetically modified (GM) foods in humans, but recent genetic research in China appears to contradict that assumption. Researchers there found the gene-regulating ribonucleic acid (RNA) of rice in the blood and organs of humans who eat it, showing that ingested genetic material can bind to humans and potentially influence their cell function. If the research survives scrutiny, it has vast implications for the future of genetically modified foods; even if it doesn't, the mere possibility of such a discovery underscores just how inadequate the biotech industry's own testing has been to date. Monsanto's refusal to study the effects of introduced DNA and RNA when ingested by humans is not only arrogant, it is potentially reckless.

Chinese researchers have found small pieces of rice ribonucleic acid (RNA) in the blood and organs of humans who eat rice. The Nanjing University-based team showed that this genetic material will bind to receptors in human liver cells and influence the uptake of cholesterol from the blood.

The type of RNA in question is called microRNA (abbreviated to miRNA) due to its small size. MiRNAs have been studied extensively since their discovery ten years ago, and have been implicated as playing roles in the mechanics of several human diseases including cancer, Alzheimer's, and diabetes. They usually function by turning down or shutting down certain genes. This isn't to say that all miRNA is dangerous—various forms of it are present in all of the food we eat. The Chinese research provides the first in vivo example of ingested plant miRNA surviving digestion and influencing human cell function in this way.

Should the research survive scientific scrutiny—a serious hurdle—it would mean that we're eating not just vitamins, protein, and fuel, but gene regulators as well. This could prove a game changer in many fields, including medicine.

It could illuminate new mechanisms behind some metabolic disorders, and perhaps explain how some herbal and modern medicines function. It could also lead to new types of medicines

This study had nothing to do with genetically modified (GM) food, but it could have implications on that front. The work shows a pathway by which new food products, such as GM foods, could influence human health in previously unanticipated ways.

The "Central Dogma" of Genetics

Monsanto's website states, "There is no need for, or value in testing the safety of GM foods in humans." This viewpoint, while good for business, rests on an understanding of genetics circa 1960. It follows what's called the "Central Dogma" of genetics, which postulates a one-way chain of command between DNA and the cells DNA governs.

The Central Dogma resembles the process of ordering a pizza. The DNA codes for the kind of pizza it wants, and orders it. The RNA is the order slip, which communicates the specifics of that pizza to the cook. The finished and delivered pizza is analogous to the protein that DNA codes for.

RNA knockdown was first used commercially in 1994 to create the Flavor Savr, a tomato with increased shelf life.

We've known for decades that the Central Dogma, though basically correct, is overly simplistic. As a case in point, MiRNAs that don't code for anything, pizza or otherwise, can travel within cells silencing genes that are being expressed. So while one piece of DNA is ordering a pizza, it could also be bombarding the pizzeria with RNA signals that can cancel the delivery of other pizzas ordered by other bits of DNA.

Researchers have been using this phenomena to their advantage in the form of small, engineered RNA strands that are essentially identical to miRNA. In a technique called RNA interference, or RNA knockdown, these small bits of RNA are used to turn off, or "knock down," certain genes.

It All Started with a Tomato

RNA knockdown was first used commercially in 1994 to create the Flavor Savr, a tomato with increased shelf life. But the technique was discovered by accident, and the tomato was already on the shelves when they figured out the mechanism at work was actually RNA interference.

In 2007, several research teams began reporting success at engineering plant RNA to kill insect predators, by knocking down certain genes. As reported in [Massachusetts Institute of Technology] MIT's *Technology Review* on November 5, 2007, researchers in China used RNA knockdown to make:

... cotton plants that silence a gene that allows cotton boll-worms to process the toxin gossypol, which occurs naturally in cotton. Bollworms that eat the genetically engineered cotton can't make their toxin-processing proteins, and they die.

And:

Researchers at Monsanto and Devgen, a Belgian company, made corn plants that silence a gene essential for energy production in corn rootworms; ingestion wipes out the worms within 12 days.

Humans and insects have a lot in common, genetically. If miRNA can in fact survive the gut then it's entirely possible that miRNA intended to influence insect gene regulation could also affect humans.

Monsanto's claim that human toxicology tests are unwarranted is based on the doctrine of "substantial equivalence." According to substantial equivalence, comparisons between GM and non-GM crops need only investigate the end products of DNA expression. New DNA is not considered a threat in any other way.

"So long as the introduced protein is determined to be safe, food from GM crops determined to be substantially equivalent is not expected to pose any health risks," reads Monsanto's website.

In other words, according to this logic, as long as the final product—the pizza, as it were—is non-toxic, the introduced DNA isn't any different and doesn't pose a problem. For what it's worth, if that principle were applied to intellectual property law, many of Monsanto's patents would probably be null and void. But if it's true that miRNA can survive digestion, any safety evaluation of a GM food should have to account for the possibility of miRNA doing unexpected things.

Applying the Research

Chen-Yu Zhang, the lead researcher on the Chinese RNA study, has made no comment regarding the implications of his work for the debate over the safety of GM food. Nonetheless, these discoveries help give shape to concerns about substantial equivalence that have been raised for years from within the scientific community.

In 1999, a group of scientists wrote a letter titled "Beyond Substantial Equivalence" to the prestigious journal *Nature*. In the letter, Erik Millstone et. al. called substantial equivalence "a pseudo-scientific concept" that is "inherently anti-scientific because it was created primarily to provide an excuse for not requiring biochemical or toxicological tests."

OECD [Organization for Economic Co-operation and Development] has helped Monsanto spread substantial equivalence globally.

To these charges, Monsanto responded: "The concept of substantial equivalence was elaborated by international scientific and regulatory experts convened by the Organization for Economic Co-operation and Development (OECD) in 1991, well before any biotechnology products were ready for market."

The Spread of Substantial Equivalence

This response is less a rebuttal than a testimonial to Monsanto's prowess at handling regulatory affairs. While the term was established before any products were ready for the market, doing so was a prerequisite to the global commercialization of GM crops. It created a legal framework for selling GM foods anywhere in the world that substantial equivalence was accepted. By the time substantial equivalence was adopted, Monsanto had already developed numerous GM crops and was actively grooming them for market.

The OECD's mission is to spread economic development to the rest of the world. And while the mission has yet to be accomplished, OECD has helped Monsanto spread substantial equivalence globally.

Many GM food supporters argue that if we have to do toxicity tests on GM foods, we should also have to do toxicity testing on every other kind of food in the world.

But we've already done the testing on the existing plants. We tested them the hard way, by eating strange things and dying, or almost dying, over thousands of years. That's how we've figured out which plants are poisonous. And over the course of each of our lifetimes we've learned which foods we're allergic to.

All of the non-GM breeds and hybrid species that we eat have been shaped by the genetic variability offered by parents whose genes were similar enough that they could mate, graft, or test tube baby their way to an offspring that resembled them.

A tomato with fish genes is another story. We shouldn't have to figure out if it's poisonous or allergenic the old fashioned way, especially in light of how new-fangled the science is.

Technology Has Outpaced Regulation

It's time to re-write the rules to acknowledge how much more complicated genetic systems are than the legal regulations—and the corporations that have written them—give credit.

Monsanto isn't doing itself any PR [public relations] favors by claiming "no need for, or value in testing the safety of GM foods in humans." Admittedly, such testing can be difficult to construct. At the same time, if companies like Monsanto want to use processes like RNA interference to create plants that can kill insects via genetic pathways that might resemble our own, some kind of testing has to happen.

A good place to start would be the testing of introduced DNA for other effects—miRNA-mediated or otherwise—beyond the specific proteins they code for. But the status quo, according to Monsanto's website, is:

There is no need to test the safety of DNA introduced into GM crops. DNA (and resulting RNA) is present in almost all foods. DNA is non-toxic and the presence of DNA, in and of itself, presents no hazard.

Given what we know, that stance is arrogant. Time will tell if it's reckless.

Genetics is turning out to be more complicated than [James] Watson and [Francis] Cricks' [who discovered the structure of DNA] Central Dogma gives credit, as groundbreaking as their research was. Given what we know now, as well as the unknown unknowns yet to be discovered, it's time for Monsanto to acknowledge that there's more to DNA than the proteins it codes for.

11

Genetically Modified Foods Have Been Studied and Found Safe to Eat

JoAnna Wendel

JoAnna Wendel is web editor for the Genetic Literacy Project, a nonprofit that explores the intersection of DNA research, media, and policy to separate science from ideology.

Many people who oppose genetically modified (GM) foods use the arguments that such foods have not been adequately studied and that there is no scientific consensus on whether they are safe. Such claims are flatly untrue. GM crops have been extensively studied and found to be as safe as—or even safer than— conventional or organic foods, and the scientific community is in broad agreement about this fact. Researchers from Italy recently analyzed more than seventeen hundred studies about the safety and environmental impacts of GM foods and found zero evidence that GM foods pose risks to humans or animals. The research review also showed that there is "little to no evidence" that GM crops negatively affect the environment. From these results, it is apparent that negative public perception about the safety of GM foods is not based on actual science.

"The science just hasn't been done."

—Charles Benbrook, organic researcher, Washington State University.

"There is no credible evidence that GMO [genetically modified organism] foods are safe to eat."

—David Schubert, Salk Institute of Biological Studies.

"[The] research [on GMOs] is scant. . . . Whether they're killing us slowly—contributing to long-term, chronic maladies—remains anyone's guess."

—Tom Philpott, *Mother Jones*.

"Genetically modified (GM) foods should be a concern for those who suffer from food allergies because they are not tested. . . ."

—Organic Consumers Association.

A popular weapon used by those critical of agricultural biotechnology is to claim that there has been little to no evaluation of the safety of GM crops and there is no scientific consensus on this issue.

Those claims are simply not true. Every major international science body in the world has reviewed multiple independent studies—in some cases numbering in the hundreds—in coming to the consensus conclusion that GMO crops are as safe or safer than conventional or organic foods, but the magnitude of the research has never been evaluated or documented.

Still the claim that GMOs are 'understudied'—the meme represented in the quotes highlighted at the beginning of this article—has become a staple of anti-GMO critics, especially activist journalists. In response to what they believed was an information gap, a team of Italian scientists cataloged and analyzed 1,783 studies about the safety and environmental impacts of GMO foods—a staggering number.

No Evidence of Harm

The researchers couldn't find a single credible example demonstrating that GM foods pose any harm to humans or animals. "The scientific research conducted so far has not detected any significant hazards directly connected with the use of genetically engineered crops," the scientists concluded.

The research review, published in *Critical Reviews in Biotechnology* in September [2013], spanned only the last decade—from 2002 to 2012—which represents only about a third of the lifetime of GM technology.

Concern about GMOs has been greatly exaggerated.

"Our goal was to create a single document where interested people of all levels of expertise can get an overview on what has been done by scientists regarding GE [genetically engineered] crop safety," lead researcher Alessandro Nicolia, applied biologist at the University of Perugia, told *Real Clear Science*. "We tried to give a balanced view informing about what has been debated, the conclusions reached so far, and emerging issues."

The conclusions are also striking because European governments, Italy in particular, have not been as embracing of genetically modified crops as has North and South America, although the consensus of European scientists has been generally positive.

The Italian review not only compiled independent research on GMOs over the last ten years but also summarizes findings in the different categories of GM research: general literature, environmental impact, safety of consumption and traceability.

Exaggerated Concerns

The "general literature" category of studies largely reveals the differences between the US, EU [European Union] and other countries when it comes to regulating GM crops. Due to lack of uniform regulatory practices and the rise of non-scientific rhetoric, Nicolia and his colleagues report, concern about GMOs has been greatly exaggerated.

Environmental impact studies are predominant in the body of GM research, making up 68% of the 1,783 studies. These studies investigated environmental impact on the crop-level, farm-level and landscape-level. Nicolia and his team found "little to no evidence" that GM crops have a negative environmental impact on their surroundings.

One of the fastest growing areas of research is in gene flow, the potential for genes from GM crops to be found— "contaminate" in the parlance of activists—in non-GM crops in neighboring fields. Nicolia and his colleagues report that this has been observed, and scientists have been studying ways to reduce this risk with different strategies such as isolation distances and post-harvest practices. The review notes that gene flow is not unique to GM technology and is commonly seen in wild plants and non-GM crops. While gene flow could certainly benefit from more research, Nicolia and his colleagues suggest, the public's aversion to field trials discourages many scientists, especially in the EU.

Allergy and DNA Fears Are Unfounded

In the food and feeding category, the team found no evidence that approved GMOs introduce any unique allergens or toxins into the food supply. All GM crops are tested against a database of all known allergens before commercialization and any crop found containing new allergens is not approved or marketed.

The researchers also address the safety of transcribed RNA [ribonucleic acid] from transgenic DNA. Are scientists fiddling with the 'natural order' of life? In fact, humans consume between 0.1 and 1 gram of DNA per day, from both GM and non-GM ingredients. This DNA is generally degraded by food processing, and any surviving DNA is then subsequently degraded in the digestive system. No evidence was found that DNA absorbed through the GI tract could be integrated into human cells—a popular anti-GMO criticism.

These 1,783 studies are expected to be merged into the public database known as GENERA (Genetic Engineering Risk Atlas) being built by Biofortified, an independent non-profit website. Officially launched in 2012, GENERA includes peer-reviewed journal articles from different aspects of GM research, including basic genetics, feeding studies, environmental impact and nutritional impact.

GENERA has more than 650 studies listed so far, many of which also show up in the new database. When merged, there should be well over 2,000 GMO related studies, a sizable percentage—as many as 1,000—that have been independently executed by independent scientists.

In short, genetically modified foods are among the most extensively studied scientific subjects in history. This year celebrates the 30th anniversary of GM technology, and the paper's conclusion is unequivocal: there is no credible evidence that GMOs pose any unique threat to the environment or the public's health. The reason for the public's distrust of GMOs lies in psychology, politics and false debates.

12

Genetically Modified Foods Need More Regulation

Food & Water Watch

Food & Water Watch is a nonprofit that advocates for public policies that will result in healthy, safe food and access to safe and affordable drinking water. The organization strongly opposes the development and use of genetically modified organisms.

Genetically modified (GM) foods have been added to the American food supply without adequate review beforehand and with a lack of post-market oversight by the regulatory agencies that are supposed to ensure they do not harm people or the environment. The US Food and Drug Administration, Department of Agriculture, and Environmental Protection Agency have all badly failed in their responsibilities to evaluate and monitor the potential risks of GM foods. The biotech industry largely regulates itself, and no independent safety testing is required by governmental agencies. Among other changes to address this situation, there should be a moratorium on approving new GM plants and animals; a new regulatory framework for biotech foods should be developed and implemented; and labels should be required for all GM crops, ingredients, and animal products.

Since the 1996 introduction of genetically engineered crops—crops that are altered with inserted genetic material to exhibit a desired trait—U.S. agribusiness and policymakers have embraced biotechnology as a silver bullet for the food system. The industry promotes biotechnology as an environmentally responsible, profitable way for farmers to feed a growing global population. But despite all the hype, genetically engineered plants and animals do not perform better than their traditional counterparts, and they raise a slew of health, environmental and ethical concerns. The next wave of the "Green Revolution" promises increased technology to ensure food security and mitigate the effects of climate change, but it has not delivered. The only people who are experiencing security are the few, massive corporations that are controlling the food system at every step and seeing large profit margins.

Additionally, a lack of responsibility, collaboration or organization from three U.S. federal agencies—the Food and Drug Administration (FDA), the U.S. Department of Agriculture (USDA) and the Environmental Protection Agency (EPA)—has put human and environmental health at risk through inadequate review of genetically engineered (GE) foods, a lack of post-market oversight that has led to various cases of unintentional food contamination and to a failure to require labeling of these foods. Organic farming, which does not allow the use of GE, has been shown to be safer and more effective than using modified seed. Moreover, public opinion surveys indicate that people prefer food that has not been manipulated or at least want to know whether food has been modified. . . .

Insufficient Protection

The patchwork of federal agencies that regulates genetically engineered crops and animals in the United States has failed to adequately oversee and monitor GE products. Lax enforcement, uncoordinated agency oversight and ambivalent post-approval monitoring of biotechnology have allowed risky GE plants and animals to slip through the regulatory cracks.

Federal regulators approve most applications for GE field trials, and no crops have been rejected for commercial cultivation. Although some biotechnology companies have withdrawn pending applications, federal regulators approve most GE crops despite widespread concerns about the risk to consumers and the environment. Nonetheless, the biotech industry has pressed for lighter regulatory oversight. Between 1999 and 2009, the top agricultural biotechnology firms spent more than $547 million on lobbying and campaign contributions to ease GE regulatory oversight, push for GE approvals and prevent GE labeling.

The USDA has approved most of the applications for biotech field releases it has received, giving the green light to 92 percent of all submitted applications between 1987 and 2005.

The current laws and regulations to ensure the health and environmental safety of biotechnology products were established before genetic engineering techniques were even discovered. The agencies responsible for regulating and approving biotechnology include the USDA, the EPA and the FDA. Although the missions of these agencies overlap in some areas, it is the responsibility of the USDA to ensure that GE crops are safe to grow, the EPA to ensure that GE products will not harm the environment and the FDA to ensure that GE food is safe to eat.

Safe to Grow?

The USDA is responsible for protecting crops and the environment from agricultural pests, diseases and weeds, including biotech and conventional crops. The Animal and Plant Health Inspection Service (APHIS) oversees the entire GE crop approval process, including allowing field testing, placing restrictions on imports and interstate shipping, approving commercial cultivation and monitoring approved GE crops.

The USDA reviews permit applications and performs environmental assessments to decide whether GE plants will pose environmental risks before field trials may begin. The USDA has approved most of the applications for biotech field releases it has received, giving the green light to 92 percent of all submitted applications between 1987 and 2005. Once field trials are complete, the USDA can deregulate a crop, allowing it to be grown and sold without further oversight. By 2008, the USDA had approved nearly 65 percent of new GE crop deregulation petitions.

Safe for the Environment?

The EPA regulates pesticides and herbicides, including GE crops that are designed to be insect resistant. A pesticide is defined as a substance that "prevents, destroys, repels or mitigates a pest," and all pesticides that are sold and used in the United States fall under EPA jurisdiction. The EPA also sets allowable levels of pesticide residues in food, including GE insect-resistant crops. Between 1995 and 2008, the EPA registered 29 GE pesticides engineered into corn, cotton and potatoes.

Bioengineered pesticides are regulated under the Federal Insecticide, Fungicide and Rodenticide Act (FIFRA), first enacted in 1947. New pesticides—including those designed for insect-resistant GE crops—must demonstrate that they do not cause "unreasonable adverse effects on the environment," including polluting ecosystems and posing environmental and public health risks. The EPA must approve and register new GE insect-resistant crop traits, just as the agency does with conventional pesticides. Biotech companies must apply to field test new insect-resistant GE crop traits, establish permissible pesticide trait residue levels for food and register the pesticide trait for commercial production.

Safe to Eat?

The FDA is responsible for the safety of both conventional and GE food, animal feed and medicines. The agency regulates GE foods under the Food, Drug and Cosmetics Act, which also gives the FDA authority over the genetic manipulation of animals or products intended to affect animals. GE foods, like non-GE foods, can pose risks to consumers from potential allergens and toxins. The FDA does not determine the safety of proposed GE foods; instead, it evaluates whether the GE product is similar to comparable non-GE products.

The biotechnology industry self-regulates when it comes to the safety of GE foods. In seeking approval, a company participates in a voluntary consultation process with the FDA, and the agency classifies the GE substances either as "generally recognized as safe" (GRAS) or as a food additive. So far, only one GE product has ever been through the more rigorous "food-additive" process; the FDA has awarded GRAS status to almost all (95 percent) of foods and traits in food since 1998. The FDA also enforces tolerances set by the EPA for pesticidal residues in food. The FDA does no independent safety testing of its own and instead relies on data submitted by biotech companies.

The FDA also regulates genetically engineered animals as veterinary medicines. In 2009, the agency decided that the Food, Drug and Cosmetics Act definition of veterinary drugs as substances "intended to affect the structure of any function of the body of man or other animals" includes genetically altered animals. As of late 2013, only GE salmon and Enviropig had been considered for commercial approval, but no transgenic animals had been approved to enter the food supply.

Impact on Consumers

Despite the FDA's approval of common GE crops, questions about the safety of eating these crops persist. GE corn and soybeans are the building blocks of the industrialized food supply, from livestock feed to hydrogenated vegetable oils to high-fructose corn syrup. Safety studies on GE foods are limited because biotechnology companies prohibit cultivation for research purposes in their seed licensing agreement.

GE insect-resistant crops may contain potential allergens.

Some of the independent, peer-reviewed research that has been done on biotech crops has revealed some troubling health implications. . . .

The potential long-term risks from eating GE food are unknown. The FDA contends that there is not sufficient scientific evidence demonstrating that ingesting these foods leads to chronic harm. But GE varieties became the majority of the U.S. corn crop only in 2005 and the majority of the U.S. soybean crop only in 2000. The potential cumulative, long-term risks have not been studied. These considerations should be critical in determining the safety of a product prior to approval, and not left to attempt to assess once the product is on the market.

GE insect-resistant crops may contain potential allergens. One harmless bean protein that was spliced onto pea crops to deter pests caused allergic lung damage and skin problems in mice. Yet there are no definitive methods for assessing the potential allergenicity of bioengineered proteins in humans. This gap in regulation has failed to ensure that potential allergenic GE crops are kept out of the food supply.

In 1998, the EPA approved restricted cultivation of Aventis' insect-resistant StarLink corn, but only for domestic animal feed and industrial purposes because the corn had not been tested for human allergenicity. However, in 2000, StarLink traces were found in taco shells in U.S. supermarkets. The EPA granted Aventis's request to cancel StarLink's registration, helping to remove the GE corn from the food supply. The

StarLink episode is a cautionary tale of the failure of the entire regulatory system to keep unapproved GE crops out of the human food supply.

Insufficient Labeling

The FDA governs the proper labeling of U.S. food products. However, because the agency views GE foods as indistinct from conventional foods, the FDA does not require the labeling of GE food products as such. The FDA does permit voluntary GE labeling as long as the information is not false or misleading. Food manufacturers can either affirmatively label GE food or indicate that the food item does not contain GE ingredients (known as "absence labeling"). Virtually no companies disclose that they are using GE ingredients under this voluntary scheme. Moreover, consumers in the United States blindly consume foods that contain GE ingredients.

For consumers to have the opportunity to make informed choices about their food, all GE foods should be labeled. A 2013 *New York Times* poll found that 93 percent of respondents were in favor of a mandatory label for genetically engineered food. A 2010 Consumers Union poll found that 95 percent of U.S. consumers favor mandatory labeling of meat and milk from GE animals. Yet despite this overwhelming support, the FDA will not require labeling of food that comes from genetically modified animals such as the AquAdvantage salmon. . . .

Policy Recommendations

The U.S. experiment with GE food has been a failure. Impacts on the environment, food system, and public health are not fully documented but are cleary not worth it. It is time for a new approach to biotechnology in the food system.

- *Enact a moratorium on new U.S. approvals of genetically engineered plants and animals.*

- *Require mandatory labeling of GE foods*: An affirmative label should be present on all GE foods, ingredients and animal products.

- *Shift liability of GE contamination to seed patent holders*: The financial responsibility of contamination should be on the patent holders of the GE technology, rather than on those who are economically harmed. The patent-holding biotechnology company should financially compensate farmers whose crops are contaminated.

- *Institute the precautionary principle for GE foods*: Currently in the United States, most GE foods, donor organisms and host organisms are generally considered safe for consumption and the environment until proven otherwise. The United States should enact policy that would more rigorously evaluate the potentially harmful effects of GE crops before their commercialization to ensure the safety of the public.

- *Develop new regulatory framework for biotech foods*: Congress should establish regulations specifically suited to GE foods.

- *Improve agency coordination and increase post-market regulation*: The EPA, USDA and FDA should create mechanisms for coordinating information and policy decisions to correct major regulatory deficiencies highlighted by the GAO [US Government Accountability Office]. Additionally, the agencies should adequately monitor the post-market status of GE plants, animals and food.

13

The FDA Effectively Regulates Genetically Modified Foods

US Food and Drug Administration

The US Food and Drug Administration (FDA) is the US government agency responsible for ensuring the quality and safety of all food and drug products sold in the United States.

The US Food and Drug Administration regulates the safety of food and food products, including genetically modified (GM) plants and animals. Foods from GM plants must meet the same safety standards as non-GM foods. Before such food is put on the market, it typically goes through a voluntary "consultation" process in which the food developer submits extensive information about its product to the FDA for review, so that any concerns about safety can be addressed before the food is sold. The agency handles GM food animals somewhat differently, using regulations that govern the use of animals to produce bioengineered drugs or organs to assess the safety of potential GM food animals as well. Because the animal-drug investigation process is exhaustive and involves strict requirements, the FDA believes it is unnecessary to create new regulations specifically to address GM animals. To date, no GM food animals have been approved by the FDA.

Question: *What is genetic engineering?*

Answer: Genetic engineering is the name for certain methods that scientists use to introduce new traits or characteristics to an organism. For example, plants may be genetically engi-

US Food and Drug Administration, "Questions & Answers on Food from Genetically Engineered Plants" and "Animal and Veterinary Genetic Engineering: General Q&A," FDA.gov, 2013.

neered [GE] to produce characteristics to enhance the growth or nutritional profile of food crops. While these technique are sometimes referred to as "genetic modification," FDA [US Food and Drug Administration] considers "genetic engineering" to be the more precise term. Food and food ingredients from genetically engineered plants were introduced into our food supply in the 1990s.

Q: *Are foods from genetically engineered plants regulated by FDA?*

A: Yes. FDA regulates the safety of foods and food products from plant sources including food from genetically engineered plants. This includes animal feed, as under the Federal Food, Drug, and Cosmetic Act, food is defined in relevant part as food for man and other animals. FDA has set up a voluntary consultation process to engage with the developers of genetically engineered plants to help ensure the safety of food from these products.

FDA regulates genetically engineered animals in a different way.

FDA considers a consultation to be complete only when its team of scientists are satisfied with the developer's safety assessment.

Q: *Are foods from genetically engineered plants safe?*

A: Foods from genetically engineered plants must meet the same requirements, including safety requirements, as foods from traditionally bred plants. FDA has a consultation process that encourages developers of genetically engineered plants to consult with FDA before marketing their products. This process helps developers determine the necessary steps to ensure their food products are safe and lawful. The goal of the con-

sultation process is to ensure that any safety or other regulatory issues related to a food product are resolved before commercial distribution. Foods from genetically engineered plants
intended to be grown in the United States that have been
evaluated by FDA through the consultation process have not
gone on the market until the FDA's questions about the safety
of such products have been resolved.

Q: *How is the safety of food from a genetically engineered plant
evaluated?*

A: Evaluating the safety of food from a genetically engineered
plant is a comprehensive process that includes several steps.
Generally, the developer identifies the distinguishing attributes
of new genetic traits and assesses whether any new material
that a person consumed in food made from the genetically
engineered plants could be toxic or allergenic. The developer
also compares the levels of nutrients in the new genetically
engineered plant to traditionally bred plants. This typically includes such nutrients as fiber, protein, fat, vitamins, and min-
erals. The developer includes this information in a safety assessment, which FDA's Biotechnology Evaluation Team then
evaluates for safety and compliance with the law.

FDA teams of scientists knowledgeable in genetic engineering,
toxicology, chemistry, nutrition, and other scientific areas as
needed carefully evaluate the safety assessments taking into
account relevant data and information.

FDA considers a consultation to be complete only when its
team of scientists are satisfied with the developer's safety assessment and have no further questions regarding safety or
regulatory issues. Please see http://www.fda.gov/biocon
inventory for a list of completed consultations.

Q: *Why do developers genetically engineer plants and which has
FDA evaluated for safety?*

A: Developers genetically engineer plants for many of the same reasons that traditional breeding is used, such as resistance to insect damage, hardiness or enhanced nutrition. As of December 2012, the FDA has completed 95 consultations, most of them on corn. . . . [As of April 1, 2013] There were 30 submissions on corn, 15 on cotton, 12 each on canola and soybean, and 24 on all other crops including alfalfa, cantaloupe, creeping bentgrass, flax, papaya, plum, potato, raddichio, squash, sugar beet, tomato, and wheat.

Q: *Which foods are made from genetically engineered plants?*

A: The majority of genetically engineered plants—corn, canola, soybean, and cotton—are typically used to make ingredients that are then used in other food products. Such ingredients include cornstarch in soups and sauces, corn syrup as a general purpose sweetener, and cottonseed oil, canola oil, and soybean oil in mayonnaise, salad dressings, cereals, breads, and snack foods.

Q: *Are foods from genetically engineered plants less nutritious than comparable foods?*

A: Nutritional assessments for foods from genetically engineered plants that have been evaluated by FDA through the consultation process have shown that such foods are generally as nutritious as foods from comparable traditionally bred plants.

Q: *Are foods from genetically engineered plants more likely to cause an allergic reaction or be toxic?*

A: The foods we have evaluated through the consultation process have not been more likely to cause an allergic or toxic reaction than foods from traditionally bred plants. When new genetic traits are introduced into plants, the developer evaluates whether any new material could be allergenic or toxic if consumed in foods made from the genetically engineered plants or from ingredients derived from these plants.

Q: *Why aren't foods from genetically engineered plants labeled?*

A: We recognize and appreciate the strong interest that many consumers have in knowing whether a food was produced using genetic engineering. Currently, food manufacturers may indicate through voluntary labeling whether foods have or have not been developed through genetic engineering, provided that such labeling is truthful and not misleading. FDA supports voluntary labeling that provides consumers with this information and has issued draft guidance to industry regarding such labeling.

The largest class of GE [genetically engineered] animals is being developed for biopharm purposes.

Q: *Are there long-term health effects of foods from genetically engineered plants?*

A: When evaluating the safety of food from genetically engineered plants, scientists with experience in assessing the long-term safety of food and food ingredients consider several factors, such as information about the long-term safety of the food from traditionally bred crops in combination with information on the food safety of the newly introduced traits. Foods from genetically engineered plants that have been evaluated by FDA through the consultation process have not gone on the market until the FDA's questions about the safety of such products have been resolved.

Q: *What kinds of GE animals are in development?*

A: Many kinds of GE animals are in development. At this time, the largest class of GE animals is being developed for biopharm purposes—that is, they are intended to produce substances (for example, in their milk or blood) that can be used as human or animal pharmaceuticals. Another group of

GE animals are under development for use as sources of scarce cells, tissues, or organs for transplantation into humans (xenotransplant sources). Yet others are intended for use as food and may be disease resistant, or have improved nutritional or growth characteristics. And others include animals that produce high value industrial or consumer products, such as highly specific antimicrobials against human and animal pathogens (e.g., *E. coli 0157* or *Salmonella*).

Q: *How are GE animals different from conventional animals?*

A: From a scientific perspective, the only intrinsic difference is that GE animals contain an rDNA [recombinant DNA] construct that gives them a new trait or characteristic, such as producing a pharmaceutical or growing faster. The degree of difference between a GE animal and its conventional counterpart will depend on the new trait that the GE animal possesses. . . .

Q: *How does the agency regulate GE animals and their products?*

A: FDA regulates GE animals under the new animal drug provisions of the Federal Food, Drug, and Cosmetic Act (FFDCA), and FDA's regulations for new animal drugs. This guidance is intended to help industry understand the statutory and regulatory requirements as they apply to these animals, including those of the National Environmental Policy Act (NEPA), to inform the public about the process FDA is using to regulate GE animals, and to gather input from the public and the regulated industry. . . .

Q: *Are GE animals "drugs"?*

A: No, GE animals are not drugs. Rather, the agency is regulating GE animals under the new animal drug provisions of the Federal Food, Drug, and Cosmetic Act (FFDCA). The

FFDCA defines a new animal drug as "an article (other than food) intended to affect the structure or any function of the body of ... animals." A recombinant DNA (rDNA) construct intended to affect the structure or function of an animal meets the definition of a new animal drug, regardless of whether the resulting GE animals are intended for food, or to produce pharmaceuticals or any other substances. . . .

Q: *Are all GE animals subject to regulation under the new animal drug provisions of the Act?*

A: Yes, any animal containing an rDNA construct intended to alter its structure or function is subject to regulation by FDA prior to commercialization. However, based on risk, there are some GE animals for which the agency may not require an approval. In general, these include laboratory animals used for research. On a case-by-case basis, the agency may consider exercising enforcement discretion for GE animals of very low risk, such as it did for an aquarium fish genetically engineered to fluoresce in the dark. The agency does not anticipate exercising enforcement discretion for any GE animal of a species traditionally consumed as food, and expects to require approval of all GE animals intended to go into the human food supply. . . .

Q: *Why is this different from the way in which GE plants are being regulated?*

A: There are a number of reasons for the difference. One overarching reason is that, unlike in some other countries, the US has not considered it appropriate to create a "novel food" regulation. That is, the US does not subject foods from GE organisms to a specific new regulation simply because of their GE status. Rather, the US has so far found that its existing laws can be applied to provide appropriate regulatory controls over GE foods. And because US law generally treats plants and animals differently, and treats food from plants differently from food from animals, the regulatory procedures for GE plants will, of necessity, differ from the regulatory procedures for GE animals.

To date, FDA has neither received requests for nor granted any food use authorizations for investigational animals containing rDNA constructs.

Another reason is that, unlike plants, animals can transmit diseases to humans, and in some very notable cases, are the origin of viral diseases in humans (e.g., swine flu). Depending on the nature of the modification to an animal, including the nature of any DNA sequences used to introduce or insert the rDNA construct into the animal, genetic engineering can enhance (or minimize) risks to human health. Although food from plants can be contaminated with human pathogens (usually from animals), and can thereby cause human illness, plants themselves ordinarily do not transmit human diseases. Genetic engineering does not change this. Therefore, GE animals can pose human health risks that would not arise with GE plants. The different regulatory approaches address these different risks. . . .

Q: *Are there GE animals in the food supply?*

A: FDA has not approved any GE animals for food (or for any other purpose). During the pre-approval investigational phase, there are strong statutory and regulatory prohibitions against unreported movement of GE animals as well as against their disposal in the food supply unless explicitly approved by the FDA. In addition, there are strict requirements for good record-keeping during the investigational phase.

FDA has been working closely with developers of GE animals to ensure that they are aware of the regulations, particularly with respect to disposition of investigational animals. . . . To date, FDA has neither received requests for nor granted any food use authorizations for investigational animals containing rDNA constructs. . . .

Q: *Will it be safe to eat the food from GE animals?*

A: FDA will only approve food from GE animals that is safe to eat. FDA's food safety evaluation will look at the same information as that recommended internationally by Codex Alimentarius in its newly adopted guideline. . . . The Codex Alimentarius Commission was created by the Food and Agriculture Organization and the World Health Organization of the United Nations to develop, among other things, internationally harmonized guidelines that can be used to ensure fair trade standards and coordinate food standards on an international basis.

Q: *Does such food have to be specially labeled?*

A: The guidance doesn't explicitly address labeling of food from GE animals. FDA does not require that food from GE animals be labeled to indicate that it comes from GE animals, just as food from GE plants does not have to be labeled to indicate it comes from GE plants. However, if food from a GE animal is different from its non-engineered counterpart, for example if it has a different nutritional profile, in general, that change would be material information that would have to be indicated in the labeling. Food marketers may voluntarily label their foods as coming from GE or non-GE animals, as long as the labeling is truthful and not misleading. . . .

Q: *How will FDA work to inform the public about new GE animals, its decisions on them, and the science behind those decisions?*

A: At present, we intend to hold public advisory committee meetings prior to any GE animal approval. We may revisit that policy in the future as we gain more experience with reviews of GE animals.

If we intend to exercise enforcement discretion with respect to specific animal lineages, we plan to post a statement describing that intent on our website.

We have developed a number of consumer-appropriate publications to help inform consumers and other stakeholders about the technology and the agency's regulations of these animals. These are available on the FDA website.

FDA's new animal drug approvals (including for GE animals) are published in the *Federal Register*, codified in the Code of Federal Regulations, and posted on its website at Animal Drugs @ FDA. Following approvals, FDA will also provide electronic access to a summary of all information (other than confidential business or trade secret information) used in FDA's decisions as part of the freedom of information summary routinely published upon approval.

Organizations to Contact

The editors have compiled the following list of organizations concerned with the issues debated in this book. The descriptions are derived from materials provided by the organizations. All have publications or information available for interested readers. The list was compiled on the date of publication of the present volume; names, addresses, phone and fax numbers, and e-mail and Internet addresses may change. Be aware that many organizations take several weeks or longer to respond to inquiries, so allow as much time as possible.

Center for Food Safety (CFS)
660 Pennsylvania Ave. SE, #302, Washington, DC   20003
(202) 547-9359 • fax: (202) 547-9429
e-mail: office@centerforfoodsafety.org
website: www.centerforfoodsafety.org

The Center for Food Safely was founded by the International Center for Technology Assessment in 1997 to evaluate new technologies being used for food production and to offer alternative methods that provide sustainable food sources. CFS opposes the commercial release of genetically engineered food products without rigorous testing to ensure their safety, contends that all genetically engineered foods should be labeled, and believes that cloned animals and genetically engineered fish should not be used in food production. The organization provides educational materials to the public and the media and suggests guidelines to policymakers. Publications and reports, including "Genetically Modified Crops and Foods: Worldwide Regulation, Prohibition and Production," can be found on the CFS website.

Council for Responsible Genetics (CRG)
5 Upland Rd., Suite 3, Cambridge, MA   02140
(617) 868-0870 • fax: (617) 491-5344
e-mail: crg@gene-watch.org
website: www.councilforresponsiblegenetics.org

The Council for Responsible Genetics works to provide accurate and current information about emerging biotechnologies so that individuals can play a more active role in shaping policies regarding these advances. Specific topics addressed by the organization include genetic determinism, cloning and human genetic manipulation, and constructing and promoting a "Genetic Bill of Rights." *Gene Watch* is the bimonthly publication of CRG; articles from this magazine as well as other reports are available on the CRG website.

Food & Water Watch (FWW)

1616 P St. NW, Suite 300, Washington, DC   20036
(202) 683-2500 • fax: (202) 683-2501
e-mail: info@fwwatch.org
website: www.foodandwaterwatch.org

Founded in 2005, Food & Water Watch is a nonprofit organization that advocates for policies that will result in healthy, safe food and access to safe and affordable drinking water. The organization believes that it is essential for shared resources to be regulated in the public interest rather than for private gain, and it strongly opposes the development and use of genetically modified organisms (GMO). FWW's website devotes a special section to the GMO issue, featuring issue briefs, fact sheets, and reports with titles such as "The Case for GE Labeling," "Agent Orange Ready Corn," and "Superweeds: How Biotech Crops Bolster the Pesticide Industry." The group's "Let Me Decide" campaign is working to build support for federal legislation to require the nationwide labeling of genetically engineered food.

Genetic Literacy Project (GLP)

933 N Kenmore St., Suite 405, Arlington, VA   22201
(571) 319-0029
e-mail: info@geneticliteracyproject.org
website: www.geneticliteracyproject.org

The Genetic Literacy Project is a nonprofit organization funded by grants from nonpartisan foundations and donations from individuals; it has no ties to—and accepts no money from—any industry or corporation. GLP believes that biotechnology can improve food security, the environment, and public health, but it also recognizes that the public often experiences science through a lens of fear and misinformation. The goal of GLP is to promote public awareness of genetics and science literacy by exploring the intersection of DNA research, media, and policy in order to separate science from ideology. The organization's website features a large collection of publications on genetically modified organisms (GMOs), including the video *Feelings, Facts, Food and GMOs* and the articles "GMOs No Longer a Pandora's Box" and "It's Not Easy Going Non-GMO, Say US Food Companies."

Greenpeace

702 H St. NW, Suite 300, Washington, DC   20001
(202) 462-1177 • fax: (202) 462-4507
e-mail: info@wdc.greenpeace.org
website: www.greenpeace.org

Greenpeace is an environmental activism organization that works to protect the environment worldwide. The group's priorities include combating climate change, deforestation, and ocean pollution. Greenpeace opposes the genetic engineering of food and contends that any genetically modified food on the market should be labeled. The group's website features a wide variety of reports, fact sheets, and news updates about the threat of genetic engineering to the environment, as well as information about its own programs and activities opposing genetically modified organisms.

Institute for Responsible Technology (IRT)

PO Box 469, Fairfield, IA   52556
(641) 209-1765 • fax: (888) 386-6075
e-mail: info@responsibletechnology.org
website: www.responsibletechnology.org

The Institute for Responsible Technology is an organization founded by author Jeffrey Smith to educate policymakers and the public about genetically modified (GM) foods and crops.

IRT investigates and reports on the risks of GM crops and their impact on health, the environment, the economy, and agriculture, as well as the problems associated with current research, regulation, corporate practices, and reporting. The IRT website features an exhaustive collection of reports, FAQs, news articles, blogs, videos, podcasts, and other publications on the topic, including the downloadable consumer pamphlet "The Non-GMO Shopping Guide."

International Bioethics Committee (IBC)
2 United Nations Plaza, Room 900, New York, NY   10017
(212) 963-5995 • fax: (212) 963-8014
e-mail: ibc@unesco.org
website: www.unesco.org/ibc

The International Bioethics Committee is a committee within the United Nations Educational, Scientific, and Cultural Organization (UNESCO). The thirty-six independent experts who make up the committee meet to ensure that human dignity and freedom are observed and respected in biotechnological advances worldwide. The biotechnology program at UNESCO seeks to strengthen research in this field in the hopes of aiding national development and worldwide socioeconomic growth. IBC has authored declarations such as the "Universal Declaration on Bioethics and Human Rights" to provide guidelines for those working in the fields of biotechnology. These declarations, as well as reports, policy briefs, newsletters, and a periodical called *A World of Science* can be viewed online.

Just Label It
1436 U St. NW, Suite 205, Washington, DC   20009
(202) 688-5834
e-mail: http://justlabelit.org/contact
website: http://justlabelit.org

Just Label It is a national nonprofit formed to advocate for the mandatory labeling of foods containing genetically modified ingredients in the United States. The group has been instrumental in gaining signatures on a petition to the US Food and Drug Administration (FDA) calling for such labeling. Written by attorneys at the Center for Food Safety, the petition was submitted in September 2011 to the FDA and to date has received over 1.2 million signatures. The petition is still available for signing on the Just Label It website, along with a selection of articles about genetically modified foods and the right-to-know movement.

Monsanto Company

800 N Lindbergh Blvd., St. Louis, MO   63167
(314) 694-1000
e-mail: www.monsanto.com/whoweare/pages/contact-us.aspx
website: www.monsanto.com

Monsanto Componay is a US-based multinational agricultural biotechnology corporation. It is the world's leading producer of the herbicide glyphosate, marketed as "Roundup," and one of the largest producers of genetically modified (GM) seeds and crops. The viewpoints section of the company's website offers information about Monsanto's positions on various issues related to GM crops and includes articles such as "Labeling Food and Ingredients Developed from GM Seed," "Safety of Biotech (GM) Crops," and "Top 10 Questions about GMO Safety." The topic area "Just Plain False" directly addresses what the company says is common misinformation about its products.

Sierra Club

85 Second St., 2nd Floor, San Francisco, CA   94105
(415) 977-5500 • fax: (415) 977-5797
e-mail: information@sierraclub.org
website: www.sierraclub.org

One of the nation's oldest environmental organizations, the Sierra Club was founded in 1892 and has been working to protect and conserve the nation's environment ever since. The Sierra Club believes that there should be a moratorium on the planting and release of genetically modified organisms (GMOs) until extensive testing has been done to ensure their safety for both humans and the environment. The Sierra Club also opposes the patenting of GMOs and the genetic code of humans. A search of the organization's website produces nearly one thousand items containing the term GMO, including policy statements, action alerts, blog posts, and in-depth articles from *Sierra*, the club's bimonthly magazine.

Union of Concerned Scientists (UCS)
2 Brattle Square, Cambridge, MA   02138-3780
(617) 547-5552 • fax: (617) 864-9405
website: www.ucsusa.org

The Union of Concerned Scientists is a membership organization of citizens and scientists who work together to promote the responsible use of science to improve the world. UCS has extensively researched and reported on the use of genetic engineering in food and plant products, as well as on the cloning of animals in the food-production chain, generally advocating a precautionary approach to the use of these products. The organization argues that more testing must be conducted before genetically modified crops and animals for food production can be considered safe and suitable for inclusion in the marketplace. The UCS website contains a food and agriculture section that examines the impacts of genetic engineering and provides additional reports and fact sheets. Available publications online include "Failure to Yield: Evaluating the Performance of Genetically Engineered Crops" and "Policy Brief: The Rise of Superweeds."

US Food and Drug Administration (FDA)
10903 New Hampshire Ave., Silver Spring, MD   20993-0002
(888) 463-6332
e-mail: www.fda.gov/AboutFDA/ContactFDA/default.htm
website: www.fda.gov

The US Food and Drug Administration is the government agency responsible for ensuring the quality and safety of all food and drug products sold in the United States. As such, the FDA has conducted extensive tests to evaluate the safety of genetically engineered (GE) foods and has issued guidelines and regulatory measures to control what types of genetically modified products make it to market. The Center for Veterinary Medicine (CVM), an office within the FDA, specifically examines the impact of GE products on animals and has also researched and reported on the cloned animals that will be used in the food industry. Reports by both the FDA and CVM can be retrieved from the FDA's website.

Bibliography

Books

Emily Anthes — *Frankenstein's Cat: Cuddling Up to Biotech's Brave New Beasts.* New York: Farrar, Straus and Giroux, 2013.

Harvey Benson — *GMO: Health Benefits of Genetically Modified Organisms.* US: EntoBees, 2013. Kindle edition.

Colin Carter, GianCarlo Moschini, and Ian Sheldon, eds. — *Genetically Modified Food and Global Welfare.* Bingley, United Kingdom: Emerald Group Publishing, 2011.

Scott Chaskey — *Seedtime: On the History, Husbandry, Politics and Promise of Seeds.* Emmaus, PA: Rodale, 2014.

Emily Eaton — *Growing Resistance: Canadian Farmers and the Politics of Genetically Modified Wheat.* Winnepeg, Canada: University of Manitoba Press, 2013.

Barry Estabrook — *Tomatoland: How Modern Industrial Agriculture Destroyed Our Most Alluring Fruit.* Kansas City, MO: Andrews McMeel, 2011.

Nina V. Fedoroff — *Mendel in the Kitchen: A Scientist's View of Genetically Modified Food.* Washington, DC: Joseph Henry Press, 2006.

Elizabeth Fitting
The Struggle for Maize: Campesinos, Workers, and Transgenic Corn in the Mexican Countryside. Durham, NC: Duke University Press, 2010.

Jane Goodall
Seeds of Hope: Wisdom and Wonder from the World of Plants. New York: Grand Central, 2014.

Wenonah Hauter
Foodopoly: The Battle Over the Future of Food and Farming in America. New York: The New Press, 2014.

Miriam Jumba
Genetically Modified Organisms: The Mystery Unraveled. Bloomington, IN: Trafford, 2010.

Frederick Kaufman
Bet the Farm: How Food Stopped Being Food. Hoboken, NJ: Wiley, 2012.

Abby Kinchy
Seeds, Science, and Struggle: The Global Politics of Transgenic Crops. Cambridge, MA: The MIT Press, 2012.

Henry Miller and Gregory Conko
The Frankenfood Myth: How Protest and Politics Threaten the Biotech Revolution. Westport, CT: Praeger, 2004.

Beiquan Mini and Ralph Scorza, eds.
Transgenic Horticultural Crops: Challenges and Opportunities. New York: Taylor & Francis, 2011.

Marion Nestle
Food Politics: How the Food Industry Influences Nutrition and Health. Berkeley, CA: University of California Press, 2013.

Robert Paarlberg and Norman Borlaug — *Starved for Science: How Biotechnology Is Being Kept Out of Africa.* Cambridge, MA: Harvard University Press, 2008.

Raj Patel — *Stuffed and Starved: The Hidden Battle for the World Food System.* Brooklyn, NY: Melville House, 2012.

Michael Pollan — *The Omnivore's Dilemma: A Natural History of Four Meals.* London, United Kingdom: Penguin, 2007.

Peter Pringle — *Food, Inc.: Mendel to Monsanto—The Promises and Perils of the Biotech Harvest.* New York: Simon & Schuster, 2005.

Marie-Monique Robin — *The World According to Monsanto.* New York: The New Press, 2012.

Rosalie Stafford — *The History of GMOs: Genetically Engineered Corn, Canola, Cotton.* Seattle, WA: Amazon Digital Services, 2012. Kindle edition.

Paul Weirich, ed. — *Labeling Genetically Modified Food.* Oxford, United Kingdom: Oxford University Press, 2007.

Periodicals and Internet Sources

Brit Amos — "Death of the Bees. Genetically Modified Crops and the Decline of Bee Colonies in North America," Global Research, August 9, 2011. www.globalresearch.ca.

Rady Ananda — "The Effects of Genetically Modified Foods on Animal Health," Global Research, December 31, 2013. www.globalresearch.ca.

Sterling Anthony — "OMG! GMOs Are a Challenge to Packaging," *Packaging World*, June 7, 2013. www.packworld.com.

Michael Antoniou, Claire Robinson, and John Fagan — "GMO Myths and Truths: An Evidence-Based Examination of the Claims Made for the Safety and Efficacy of Genetically Modified Crops," Earth Open Source, June 2012. www.earthopensource.org.

Laura Beans — "Catholic Church Endorses GMOs as Cure for World Hunger," EcoNews, June 26, 2013. http://ecowatch.com.

Charles M. Benbrook — "Impacts of Genetically Engineered Crops on Pesticide Use in the U.S.—the First Sixteen Years," *Environmental Sciences Europe*, vol. 24, no. 24, 2012. www.enveurope.com.

Juhie Bhatia — "Africa's Hunger Hardships Spur Biotech Debate," Pulitzer Center Global Voices Online, July 21, 2010. http://pulitzercenter.org.

William Bowles   "Genetic Engineering Companies Promised Reduced Pesticide Use . . . But GMO Crops Have Led to a 25% Increase in Herbicide Use," Investigating the New Imperialism, January 27, 2014. http://williambowles.info.

Michelle Castillo   "Study Says Genetically Modified Corn Causes Tumors, but Other Scientists Skeptical About Research," CBS News, September 21, 2012. www.cbsnews.com.

Dan Charles   "In a Grain of Golden Rice, a World of Controversy Over GMO Foods," National Public Radio, March 7, 2013. www.npr.org.

Chicago Tribune   "GMO Primer: How Genetically Modified Foods Are Used, Regulated, Labeled and Avoided," January 3, 2014.

Andy Coghlan   "Is Opposition to Golden Rice 'Wicked'?" *Slate*, October 20, 2013. www.slate.com.

Economist   "Food Fight: A Fierce Public Debate Over GM Food Exposes Concerns About America," December 14, 2013.

Jon Entine   "White House Ends Its Interference in a Scientific Review," *Slate*, December 21, 2012. www.slate.com.

| Dan Fagin | "Why We Should Accept GMO Labels," *Scientific American*, October 24, 2013. |

| Food & Water Watch | "Fact Sheet: How GM Crops Hurt Farmers," February 2013. www.foodandwaterwatch.org. |

| David H. Freedman | "The Truth About Genetically Modified Food," *Scientific American*, vol. 309, no. 3, August 20, 2013. |

| Glenn Garvin | "The Left's Science Deniers," *The Miami Herald*, March 2, 2013. |

| Annie Gasparro | "General Mills Starts Making Some Cheerios Without GMOs," *Wall Street Journal*, January 2, 2014. |

| Carey Gillam | "Pesticide Use Ramping Up as GMO Crop Technology Backfires: Study," Reuters, October 1, 2012. www.reuters.com. |

| Hugh Grant | "Let's End World Hunger," Reuters, January 25, 2012. http://blogs.reuters.com. |

| Mark Guarino | "No More GMOs in Cheerios. Will a Lot More Foods Go GMO-Free Now?" *Christian Science Monitor*, January 3, 2014. |

| Amy Harmon | "A Lonely Quest for Facts on Genetically Modified Crops," *New York Times*, January 4, 2014. |

Tamar Haspel — "Genetically Modified Foods: What Is and Isn't True," *Washington Post*, October 15, 2013.

Toni Hayes — "Studies Show Genetically Modified Foods Are Not Safe for Human Consumption," Examiner.com, January 15, 2013.

Maryam Henein — "What Is Monsanto Doing to Our Bees?" Honey Colony, 2014. www.honeycolony.com.

Beth Hoffman — "Genetic Engineering; A Food Fix?" *Forbes*, August 30, 2012.

Beth Hoffman — "Golden Rice and GMOs: The Best Solutions to World Hunger?" *Forbes*, August 31, 2013.

Nathanael Johnson — "The Genetically Modified Food Debate: Where Do We Begin?" *Grist*, July 8, 2013. http://grist.org.

Nathanael Johnson — "The GM Safety Dance: What's Rule and What's Real?" *Grist*, July 10, 2013. http://grist.org.

Nathanael Johnson — "Genetic Engineering vs. Natural Breeding; What's the Difference?" *Grist*, July 16, 2013. http://grist.org.

Nathanael Johnson — "Genetic Engineering: Do the Differences Make a Difference?" *Grist*, July 24, 2013. http://grist.org.

Nathanael Johnson — "Genetically Engineered Food: Allergic to Regulations?" *Grist*, July 30, 2013. http://grist.org

Nathanael Johnson — "Golden Rice: Fool's Gold or Golden Opportunity?" *Grist*, August 29, 2013. http://grist.org.

Arvind Kumar — "Are GMOs Killing Off Bees All Over the World?" DNA India, November 26, 2013. www.dnaindia.com.

Robin McKie — "GM Food: We Can No Longer Afford to Ignore Its Advantages," *The Guardian*, October 13, 2012.

Monsanto Company — "An Overview of the Safety and Advantages of GM Foods," 2013. www.monsanto.com.

Madeline Nash — "Grains of Hope," *Time*, August 7, 2000.

Nature — "Research on Transgenic Crops Must Be Done Outside Industry If It Is to Fulfill Its Early Promise," May 2, 2013.

Robyn O'Brien — "MIT Report Links Chemical Used on Genetically Engineered Foods to Cancer and Infertility," Allergy Kids Foundation, April 27, 2013. www.allergykids.com.

Kathleen O'Neil — "World's Growing Population Will Need Crops Engineered to Produce More and Tolerate Climate Change," American Association for the Advancement of Science, July 9, 2013. www.aaas.org.

Mehmet Oz   "Give (Frozen) Peas a Chance—and
                         Carrots Too," *Time*, December 3,
                         2012.

Robert Paarlberg   "The World Needs Genetically
                         Modified Foods," *Wall Street Journal*,
                         April 14, 2013.

Katherine Paul   "Monsanto's GMO Feed Creates
                         Horrific Physical Ailments in
                         Animals," AlterNet, August 9, 2013.
                         www.alternet.org.

Tom Philpott   "Are Genetically Modified Foods Safe
                         to Eat?" *Mother Jones*, September 30,
                         2011.

Reinhard   "Golden Rice Can End World
Renneberg   Hunger," *South China Morning Post*,
                         September 23, 2012. www.scmp.com.

John Robbins   "Are Genetically Altered Foods the
                         Answer to World Hunger?" *Earth
                         Island Journal*, Winter 2002.
                         www.earthisland.org.

John Robbins   "Can GMOs Help End World
                         Hunger?" *Huffington Post*, August 1,
                         2011. www.huffingtonpost.com.

*Scientific   "Labels for GMO Foods Are a Bad
American*   Idea," September 6, 2013.

Katherine Smith   "GM Food Will Be Essential for a
                         Hungry World," *The Age*, November
                         7, 2013.

Nicola Smith   "GMOs Seen as Playing Major Role in Battling World Hunger," *Valley News*, August 5, 2013.

Mohammed   "Ghana: Genetically Modified Foods
Suleman   Are Safe to Eat—Scientist," All Africa, October 5, 2012. http://allafrica.com.

Katherine   "GMOs Are a Grand Experiment on
Tallmadge   Health, Environment," Live Science, July 10, 2013. www.livescience.com.

Josh Trebach   "Genetically Modified Foods Need Government Regulation," *Collegiate Times*, September 13, 2010. www.collegiatetimes.com.

Bryan Walsh   "Modifying the Endless Debate Over Genetically Modified Crops," *Time*, May 14, 2013.

Emily Waltz   "GM Crops: Battlefield," *Nature*, September 2, 2009.

Web MD   "Are Biotech Foods Safe to Eat?" 2013. www.webmd.com.

Jennifer Welsh   "Genetically Engineered Salmon Is Perfectly Safe, FDA Says," *Business Insider*, December 28, 2012. www.businessinsider.com.

Michael Wines   "Mystery Malady Kills More Bees Heightening Worry on Farms," *New York Times*, March 28, 2013.

World Health   "20 Questions on Genetically
Organization   Modified Foods," 2014. www.who.int.

Sasha J. Wright   "Why the GMO Debate Misses the Point," *Popular Science*, October 29, 2013. www.popsci.com.

Index

CPSIA information can be obtained
at www.ICGtesting.com
Printed in the USA
FFOW04n1508230215
11296FF

6

Genetically Modified Crops Have Created a "Superweed" Problem

Union of Concerned Scientists

The Union of Concerned Scientists (UCS) is a membership organization of citizens and scientists who work together to promote the responsible use of science to improve the world. UCS has extensively researched the use of genetic engineering in food and plant products. The organization argues that more testing must be conducted before genetically modified crops and food animals can be considered safe.

One of the biggest unintended consequences of genetically modified (GM) crops is the "superweed" problem. Weeds that grow in fields of GM crops engineered to be resistant to the herbicide glyphosate—such as Monsanto Company's Roundup Ready corn, soybeans, and other crops—have themselves become resistant to the herbicide and have infested more than sixty million acres of US cropland. Twenty-four species of weeds are now glyphosate resistant. This means that different, and often stronger, herbicides must be applied to kill the crop-choking superweeds and that new crop varieties must be engineered to withstand those new herbicide treatments. This self-perpetuating cycle is a disaster for the environment. Significantly curbing herbicide use and promoting sustainable weed-control methods should be a priority for regulatory agencies.

In what may sound like science fiction but is all too real, "superweeds" are over-running America's farm landscape, immune to the herbicides that used to keep crop-choking weeds largely in check. This plague has spread across much of the country—some 60 million acres of U.S. cropland are infested—and it is wreaking environmental havoc, driving up farmers' costs and prompting them to resort to more toxic weed-killers.

How did this happen? It turns out that big agribusiness, including the Monsanto Company, has spent much of the last two decades selling farmers products that would ultimately produce herbicide-resistant weeds. And now that thousands of farmers are afflicted with this problem, those same companies are promising new "solutions" that will just make things worse.

Overall pesticide use is an estimated 404 million pounds greater than if Roundup Ready crops had not been planted.

Herbicide-resistant weeds are also symptomatic of a bigger problem: an outdated system of farming that relies on planting huge acreages of the same crop year after year. This system, called monoculture, has provided an especially good habitat for weeds and pests and accelerated the development of resistance. In response, Monsanto and its competitors are now proposing to throw more herbicides at resistant weeds, an approach that ignores the underlying biology of agricultural systems and will inevitably lend to more resistance and a further spiraling up of herbicide use.

What is needed instead is support for approaches—which already work and are available now—that target the problem at its source. Scientists and farmers alike have developed, tested, and refined methods of growing crops that reduce the likelihood of resistance in the first place, while providing many other benefits for consumers, the environment, and farmers themselves.

Unfulfilled Promises

Monsanto first introduced its line of "Roundup Ready" seeds in the mid-1990s. These crops—which now include corn, soybeans, cotton, canola, alfalfa, and sugar beets—are genetically engineered to be immune to the company's Roundup herbicide (glyphosate). This convenient system enabled farmers to plant these seeds and later spray fields with Roundup to kill any weeds that might compete with the crops. The seeds were expensive, but in the early days farmers enthusiastically adopted them because they saved time and made weed control easier.

This system was heralded as an environmental breakthrough. Using it was supposed to make farming safer: because Roundup was widely thought to be more effective than other common herbicides and not as toxic, less total herbicide would be needed. Advocates claimed that Roundup would reduce soil loss through erosion, given that farmers would not need to plow (till) their fields as much to control weeds.

For several years, Monsanto's system did seem to work as intended. But after a temporary reduction, herbicide use on U.S. farms has increased dramatically because of growing weed resistance to Roundup; given that other chemical agents also have to be employed, overall pesticide use is an estimated 404 million pounds greater than if Roundup Ready crops had not been planted. Farmers' costs are rising, moreover, and the short-term benefit of reduced soil erosion is being reversed because farmers facing resistant weeds often find they need to till again.

What Went Wrong?

At present, more than 15 years after farmers began growing Roundup Ready crops, the most widely grown U.S. commodity crops are glyphosate-resistant, and farmers douse at least 150 million acres with the herbicide every year. As a result of this heavy use, weeds showing resistance to glyphosate began appearing in fields more than a decade ago—first as occasional interlopers but eventually as large infestations. A recent survey revealed that almost 50 percent of surveyed farms were infested with glyphosate-resistant weeds, and the rate of these weeds' spread has been increasing. Twenty-four species of weed are now glyphosate-resistant.

The worst cases are in the southeastern United States, where a reported 92 percent of cotton and soybean fields are infested as a result of Roundup Ready crops. The now-resistant Palmer amaranth (*Amaranthus palmeri*), for example, is a fast-growing weed that can reach eight feet in height, outcompeting soybeans or cotton; it develops a tough stem that can damage farm machinery and must sometimes be removed by hand—an expensive proposition. Resistant ragweeds (*Artemisia* species), marestail (*Conyza canadensis*), and water hemp (*Amaranthus tuberculatus*) are also aggressive weeds, spreading through the Midwest and the Corn Belt. Meanwhile, farmers in the Great Plains are confronting resistant populations of kochia (*Kochia scoparia*), a weed adapted to drier climates.

The situation, alarming as it is, could get a lot worse. Survey data show that in the absence of enlightened intervention, *most* U.S. farms from the Great Plains to the East Coast will become infested with resistant superweeds. Can industry help reverse the damage it has wrought?

Solutions Will Create New Problems

Farmers desperately need sustainable solutions to the escalating weed resistance problem, but the pesticide and seed industry's answer is a new generation of herbicide-resistant crops, mostly corn and soybeans, that does not address the inherent drawbacks of monoculture and current biotech crops. And this next generation is engineered to withstand not just